CRIMINAL
TO
CORNERSTONE

Charles Elwyn

ISBN 978-1-63874-852-6 (paperback)
ISBN 978-1-63874-853-3 (digital)

Christian Faith Publishing, Inc.
832 Park Avenue
Meadville, PA 16335
www.christianfaithpublishing.com

Printed in the United States of America

Author's Note

Over the years, people have pleaded with me to write this book. Well, here it is: the good, the bad, the dark, and the luminous light. This book tells my journey from childhood innocence through my involvement with the Mafia and beyond. It describes my evolution from being a criminal to a Christian. Some names have been changed to protect the innocent and relatives of the people that are mentioned.

Since my involvement with crime happened over forty years ago, I admit that perhaps some of my memories may be slightly cloudy. However, I lived this life, and as I feel called to help others, I avow that the events and conversations I've described are true.

My intention with telling my story is not to glorify my actions or my past but to give the reader a solid example that anyone can be forgiven of their past by a God who loves us all.

Contents

Acknowledgments

For the untold hours of editing and note-making, my heartfelt thanks to my good friends Hal and Gail Fandl. They are gifts from God in my life for thirty years. Also, a special thanks to Alison Montgomery, who I have known for only two years, but who has dedicated so much time and knowledge in helping me with the editing and cover art. Also, Jim Squires, who is a current friend and neighbor with enormous talent, did the final editing for me. Without them, this book would have never been completed. They are friends that have brought me so much joy with their friendship over the years.

I am also exceedingly grateful to God for the affirmation and support from my sister Patricia Elwyn, Robert Denny, Cynde Chaffin, Eileen Richardson, and Pastor Bob Cote. From conception to completion of this book, these dear ones believed.

There are so many more people throughout the years who have suggested that I write this book after hearing my testimony at pastors' conferences, men's retreats, churches, prisons, homeless shelters, and youth detention centers in multiple states throughout the west and Mexico.

Book Overview

This book has three main sections:

The first part is about my youth, and the way that I was brought up. We were very poor, and I had a father that was emotionally and verbally abusive, just to me but not to my two sisters. He was abusive to the degree that I ran away to Hell's Kitchen (NYC) in 1962 at the age of fourteen. I desire to show the reader that it is their responsibility as parents to raise their children with love and concerned attention so that the kids don't evolve into criminals like I did.

The next section is about my life as a businessman and criminal as I became "connected" to the Genovese Mafia Family. Hopefully the violence and life-threatening experiences will show the reader (of all ages) that although I had lots of money and possessions, I was miserable, hating life because of who I had become, and how I neglected my wife and my children.

The last section is the most important to me, and I hope to the reader. It shows how I came very close to killing a man, but God intervened with a *personal miracle* while building a church in San Diego. That appearance of God not only stopped me from committing a murder, but more importantly, it set me on a course of wanting to know God. I turned from being a devout atheist, as I was brought up to be, to searching for and coming to believe in God. As an atheist, I didn't care if I lived or died and asked myself, *Why not be a criminal?* This all leads to my acceptance of Jesus as my Lord and Savior, being forgiven for my life of crime and continual sinning against man and God.

As a born-again believer, I have spoken in numerous churches, youth detention centers, prisons, and homeless shelters, in seven western states and Mexico. Throughout these testimonies, I have been continually asked to write a book since God has used me in an untold number of lives to bring them to a belief in Jesus.

Lastly, after each sharing of my life of crime to forgiveness, men have come to me, telling me that they didn't think that God would accept them because of their sins. But after hearing my testimony of crime and sin, and my being accepted by God, they could see that they also could believe and be born again and forgiven of their sins and accepted into His Love and Kingdom.

Hebrew Proverb

There is an old Hebrew proverb I once heard my pastor tell. A home-owner wanted to sell his house for two thousand dollars, but the proposed buyer could only pay one thousand. The seller agreed to sell the house for one thousand under the stipulation that he could remain the sole owner of just one nail over the front entry door. He gave all kinds of excuses like it was put there by a loved one, and he wanted to be assured that it was never removed for sentimental reasons. The buyer agreed. After some time, the seller hung a rotting, smelly carcass on the door header nail that, per their agreement, the new owner could not remove because of his agreement of sole ownership. The new owner was so frustrated he chose to move out or sell the property back to the original owner for next to nothing to escape the predicament.

The moral to the story is never give Satan one small opportunity or he will enslave you forever. All he needs is a small nail in your life to own and control you.

That's how it all starts with sin. One wrong word or a stolen piece of Bazooka Bubble Gum and the next becomes easier and usually bigger. That's how it happened to me. The desire to have more by doing the bare minimum is not the way God intended. But it can drive us all, even the fairest of heart, to sin.

My Opening Statement

I've often said that at one time I walked with and respected men I thought of as kings. That is the kings of the underworld or more specifically, men of the Genovese crime syndicate. Men like the lieutenant and underboss, Anthony ("Hicky") DiLorenzo. Men like Johnny "Dio" Dioguardian, Phillip (the Brush), Salli (The Gent), "Jackie the Nose," Jerry (Moon), and a good friend Mersh, to name a few.

How well did I know these men? Well, I worked closely with them daily. Was I associated with this family? Yes, but I was not a member or even an associate of the family. I have no Italian blood in me that I know of, and you must be 100 percent Italian blood to be a family member. Members of a family were initiated into the family in a formal induction and were thereafter considered "made." Associates worked with made members under the family's direction. Hangers-on helped the organization but were neither members nor associates.

I was just a New Jersey farm town kid who ran away from home at the age of fourteen and proved that I could survive in Hell's Kitchen, NYC, on my own, for a short period of time, and often for years later. However, surviving on your own in Hell's Kitchen at the age of fourteen in 1962 goes beyond survival. It was a real education that formed memories for life. I then moved in with my Aunt Marie and Uncle Wick. I used to go to the city often on weekends to continue to be the member of a gang who called themselves "The Park Rats."

Later I wound up being involved with, and eventually respected by, known criminals in New York City. When I say I walked with them, I really mean I was indirectly involved with them. I worked primarily in the airfreight trucking industry, dealing with the Teamsters union, with airfreight companies like Emery Air Freight, Air Express International, and other airfreight forwarders. My companies did deliveries in Manhattan, Bronx, Brooklyn, Westchester County, NY, Fairfield County, Connecticut, Orange County, NY. The pickup and delivery services included all the major airlines, Eastern Lufthansa, American, Delta, TWA, United, PSA and more.

I was part of the decision-making machinery that was needed to increase production and profit in the trucking business. I was a witness and contributor to the negotiations of opposing (union) sides as well as other trucking companies. Later, I played an important part in the collection of money owed to loan sharks in the streets of NYC. And I can't forget I helped the underboss (of the Genovese crime family) escape from being imprisoned years later brought him cash in South America. Finally, and most importantly, I left my involvement in 1978 and stayed alive!

Now let me explain who these men were. I say were…because I believe they're all dead and I'm the only one alive from the group that I was associated with. Additionally, although they were all known men, that doesn't mean that they were all MAFIA. And that includes me. I was involved with them however, as explained above, not what is called a "made man, such as Anthony, Jonny Dio, and others I knew."

The first thing I want the reader to know is what the name MAFIA originally stood for, because it was a principled organization in the beginning. The origin of the word "MAFIA" began with the French invasion of Sicily in 1282, and the Italian saying, "Morte Alla Francia Italia Anela! (MAFIA)" translated, which means "Death to the French is Italy's cry!"

It was a secret organization operating mainly in Sicily, known for its intimidation of and retribution against corrupt French and Italian law enforcement officials and witnesses that approved of their activities. However, as the Mafia leaders gained more and more expansion and control of the country and its leaders it became a corrupt group. Later it became a secret criminal organization operating mainly in the United States and Italy. The mafia became known for its illegal activities such as gambling, drug-dealing, protection, prostitution, and loan sharking (to name a few). Its primary activities are protection racketeering and the intercession of disputes in criminal markets.

In reference to a man, a *mafioso* was or is ambiguous, signifying a bully: arrogant but also fearless, proud, and enterprising. These men are often full of boldness, bravado, aggressiveness, and when necessary, violence. It was also important to know when to keep your mouth shut, which is *one* of the reasons I am still alive. However, since I am not Italian, I was never part of the MAFIA, only as mentioned associated with, or better yet "associated" with jobs to do.

I also want to share an opinion that many people may not agree with. When I was associated with men who were part of the Genovese Mafia, I found them, in general, to be men who loved their family, and friends. I was never ordered or requested to do any collections on innocent persons like they show on TV or the movies, nor did I ever hear of any actions like that with anyone I was associated with. We stuck together and watched one another's backs when needed. There were absolutely no drugs sales or consumption of, or you would find yourself trying to swim in the East River with your hands tied behind your back and cement blocks on your feet. There were rules and the most important was secrecy. Just keep your mouth shut and do your job so everyone could have an income, and hopefully build a financially lucrative future.

So why did a kid like me (or maybe a kid you know), want to be part of this life? Maybe it was arrogance, since you were known to be with them, and it gave us notoriety that I'd never imagined possible. There's a certain thrill to just walking out of a club in the middle of the early morning and not knowing if you're going to get hit (killed) even by the people that you're associated with, close friends with, or maybe even related to. This is, by the way, is how Anthony "Hickey" DiLorenzo died, which will be covered later.

I was uneducated beyond high school, but boy was I resourceful! I was extremely good at what I did in all venues, providing me with a large house, new cars, furs for my wife and jewelry for us both, and custom-tailored suits and fine clothing. Also, we could afford whatever we needed to or just chose to give to our children. Although I later learned that these things didn't mean happiness for me and especially not for my wife during my time with them. As a matter of fact, I believe that it was my involvement that caused our separation and ultimately our divorce. When she married me, I was a somewhat respectable carpenter, but she wound up being married to an angry, arrogant, rude, secretive, and adulterous husband.

I refuse to use the real names of people that I was associated with. Other than the men first mentioned in the beginning of this book. Because I believe that the families of the criminals and those that I was associated with, don't deserve to be punished because of things that I or their family members chose to do.

Part of why I'm still alive was my ability to keep silent, but at the same time to know what to say, when, how, where, and to whom. I still believe that that is the way to live. I believed that those acts meant integrity, and still do. As you read on you'll see the things that I was good at, the things that I was respected for, the things that I hated with a passion, and the experiences that furthered my standing with some of the men in charge of the Genovese crime family in the New York area. I'll detail my involvement in the trucking and air freight business at Kennedy Airport, times of happiness, sadness, hatred, love, and eventually (thank God) CHANGE. Also, I was gifted much more *life* because of that change. I will explain how I changed, who I am now, and why that matters to me, my family and hopefully to YOU. To you meaning to anyone who believes that getting rich by illegal means is a good thing or is already involved in a gang or worse.

Something to remember is that my involvement was personal and again very secretive. I mention that because a great deal of my life back then was very secretive and had to be. Hence, even the people including family and friends will be surprised at many of the experiences of what I write. To be associated with the crime family it was necessary to keep secrets from my/our physical family and close friends. If I hadn't, I wouldn't be here to write this somewhat autobiography or better said life of crime, and metamorphosis into love and peace. That does not mean that they didn't know who I was involved with. In fact, there is one time that much of my family was with me and totally frightened because of an unexpected FBI raid on my home during a celebration. That is all explained in another chapter in this book, along with other experiences, including those that changed my life from hatred and crime, to love and compassion.

My wife's father, Anthony "Hickey" DiLorenzo, was known as a "made" member of the Genovese crime family by anyone and everyone since he had spent nearly half of his life in prison. Additionally, the newspapers and magazines had articles concerning not only showing his position as an "underboss" of the mafia, but how the government had found him guilty of crimes that he was going to be and was put in prison for. However, if people even family weren't surprised of the obvious involvements, no one would have known anything about him, because he kept every action or decision in secrecy from everyone, who didn't need to know. Secrecy is how his or should I say their lives help to be kept out of prison. Yes, he was imprisoned for his actions, but it wasn't because he shared his illegal activities with anyone. In fact, I believe every one of his family and friends knew him as a generous, friendly, and loving man. I learned to love him like a father.

DRIVEN

My Youth

The Bible starts off with "In the beginning, God." It's the beginning of what God has to say to us in His word and it's either the start of life with His direction and blessings or not. Before you judge what I have just said, read on to see my explanation of my life that was and what it is now.

Okay, the first thing that I want the reader to know is the reason why I am writing about my youth. Is to hopefully show what can happen to your kids if you raise them like I was raised by my father. Although I think of my mother as a saint, my father's abuse is what eventually caused me to hate life.

My life began in a world pretty much without God as instruction or belief in His son Jesus. My father many times had stated his belief in life and death at the dinner table to myself, my mother, and my two sisters. His belief was that hell is being on earth because of all its troubles, hurts, pains, wars and disasters we have to deal with. Heaven is when you die because there is nothing…no pain or sickness, no troubles or disasters, no nothing…just a body decaying in the ground that has ended living in hell on earth. And guess what? I believed him and lived my life accordingly until I was shown an absolute miracle at the age of thirty-three that put me on a track to see if there really was a God.

But let me regress a bit and give some other information about my parents. Although they were not "religious," followers of Jesus, or any other faith, they taught us to have morals such as: don't steal, treat persons with respect, respect your elders and parents, don't be a false witness, don't lie or cheat, and of course to kill would be a major no-no. And in general, I believed in these morals as truths, but as the years went on, I saw how life became unfair because of our poverty.

I held on to my father's opinion of heaven and hell and dropped the morals to enhance my life as long as I was on this earth. This form of belief also made me live a life of not caring if I lived or died. I often hear people say that everyone at some time prays to *a god* when they are in a precarious, or life-threatening condition. Atheists do exist because I was one and never even thought of a connection to a god. Even when my life was in jeopardy, I never considered praying for help.

Again, my father had a major part in this because of the life I saw him live and how he treated me. Now let me be very clear to anyone who is reading this that this is not a "poor me" or "I blame my dad for everything in my life" scenario. I have grown to love my dad, not like him, but love him as a father, a sinner, and a lost person who never learned, sought, or believed the truth about life, about God and about His son Jesus who died for him. That's a decision that each of us must make before we die with the decision, as my father did.

We used to believe that my father was an alcoholic because of all the beer and booze he would consume. Although fortunately he stopped drinking on his own in his seventies. He drank so much beer and threw so many parties that he had a delivery of several cases of Horlacher beer to the house on a weekly or biweekly schedule. I am not sure which came first, the driver of the Piels delivery truck becoming a friend and drinking partner of my fathers who went by the nickname of "Beaky," or was Beaky, a friend prior to the deliveries of the cases of beer. He was most likely also an alcoholic, but a great guy to me. I have no bad memories of him other than I was almost killed in a car accident at the age of fourteen years old while he was driving. But that wasn't his fault.

My dad was also a womanizer and adulterer. I can't remember ever hearing my parents having a heated or loud fight about anything. I later realized that it was because my mom loved and believed in him so much that she just gave her life to him. She denied that he was an adulterer even though we three kids always knew it and, later as we got older, used to tease her about it because of her denial of the truth.

There is a Proverb (#31) in the Bible that best describes my mother, as a wife, a provider, and a respected woman by those who knew her including us kids.

She was the one who had a steady job as an accountant for all the years I knew her. She wasn't certified as a CPA or anything but she was a wizard with numbers, laws, and IRS statutes throughout her life. She died at the age of eighty-seven years old and had just completed helping us file our taxes for that year (2012). Both my mother and father died within two weeks of one another in September of 2012. My father died in his bed while living in Lake Clear Junction, NY, where they used to live together before they separated. Two weeks later, my mother died also in her bed while under the care of my two sisters, while living with my sister in Santa Fe, NM. My mother finally caught him in an adulterous relationship, and although she left him some twenty or more years ago, she wouldn't divorce him because she still loved him. When she learned that he had died, she decided to die and did so two weeks later. Us kids, who at that time were in our sixties, believed that she didn't want to live without him on this earth, even though he lived 2,100 miles away.

My father had been raised as a farmer most of his life in a very rural farm area that I visited one day when I was a young boy. What I remember is riding for a very long time on dirt roads to get to this isolated farmhouse in the middle of nowhere. I mention this only because I have always reminded myself that everyone's surroundings play a major part in who they are, especially me. He had five siblings—two brothers and three sisters. Think about that household. Six kids stranded together on a farm in the middle of nowhere. Maybe there was some strict upbringing with lots of work, and the story about walking miles to school in the snowy blizzard does easily come to mind. How can I judge my dad for just about anything until I have walked in his shoes and learned his lessons? The old saying of "you learn what you live" comes to mind. He probably thought that the way he treated me was the best because that's the way he was brought up and didn't know any better.

When I was first born, the last of three, we were living in an aging rundown apartment on the second floor next to a working railroad line in Northvale, NJ. I remember my father telling me a story. One day, my mother came into the bedroom where I was lying in a cradle and she was shocked to find a large rat licking the milk off my face. As the story goes, my dad got his .22 rifle and shot the rat in my crib fearing that if he tried to shoo it away, it might bite me. I think that was the beginning of my love for animals and adrenaline.

My sisters said that they had never heard that story, but he was the one who told me. As for the adrenaline? My mother's sister Marie had a husband named Charles Wickenden. Everybody called him Wick. He was holding me as a toddler while walking down the stairs that went from that second-floor apartment one day when he tripped and fell forward down the stairs. While holding me, he toppled onto my grandmother's back who was in front of him going down the stairs also. Our weight pushed her down the stairs, and Wick, try-ing to keep from hurting her, managed to stumble backward. Uncle Wick tells the story saying that when he finally caught himself and stopped the fall, I said to him, "Do it again!" I apparently loved the action, and this was an early example of my love of adrenaline. I have loved the feeling of increased adrenaline all my life and have lived to achieve it.

As mentioned, my uncle, Charles Wickenden, was called "Wick." We children called him Uncle Wick. What a character he was. He served in the air force during WWII as a belly gunner on a bomber that went into and over Germany several times. He never talked about it, and later we believe he had what is known today as PTSD. Marie looked like the fifties actress Jane Russell to me. They stayed in love all their lives. Uncle Wick died at the ripe age of eighty-four back in 2003 and Aunt Rie (Marie) died at the age of eighty-seven in 2010. They had no children and never really knew why they couldn't.

But I do! It was because God planned it that way for me and my sisters. They were our pseudo parents who took us everywhere and did everything with us. They gave us praise, taught us so much in our lives, including how much they loved us. My Aunt Marie was the most perfect example of love that I have ever experienced as a boy or as a man. I still often say her name was "Love."

When I was about five years old, I was traveling in a car with my mother and her friend and daughter while the friend was driving. It was raining very hard and I was in the back seat with my mother's friend's little girl who was the same age as me. I don't remember much about how it happened other than what I had been told, of course. Apparently, we came upon an area where some roadwork was being done with large equipment in the road. The warning signs weren't visible until it was too late, due to the heavy rain. When she saw the large equipment and slammed on her brakes, we kept sliding. At the last moment, she turned hard to the right side going off the road and down a very muddy slope. The car rolled over before coming to a stop on its top. Back then there were no seat belts in the cars, so all four of us were thrown around like rag dolls until the rolling stopped. At that time, we were in all kinds of positions as the road construction workers pried open the doors to help us get out.

I only mention this because we never went to a hospital! We were taken to a local police station. I remember sitting there with an enormous headache, cuts, and lots of bruised areas looking at the little girl that was in the back seat with me crying intensely while in her mother's arms. I was also sitting in my mother's lap, trying to remember what had happened to get us where we were. The husband of my mothers' friend and the little girl's father came and picked us up. He drove us to our home and left I thought for theirs. My mother cleaned us up and bandaged any bleeding areas and put me in bed to take a nap. I believe that this was the first of the six concussions I have had in my life. However, no one even thought of such a condition back then.

We were dirt poor, and since we had no insurance for the hospital, it wasn't an option. The other woman and her little girl were taken to a hospital by her father. She was okay, but they thought that she may have had a possible concussion.

As I said earlier, my father was a beer drinker. In fact, in those days, he pretty much had an alcoholic lifestyle. I'll talk about that later. He was prone to throwing card games, or just drinking parties often. These parties typically lasted well into next morning before breaking up. When the beer in the kitchen refrigerator was drank up, he would come into our bedroom (the three of us kids shared a small room together) and wake me up. He'd tell me to stock up the beer. I would then go through the kitchen to the cellar stairs, go down into the cellar with empty bottles and return with a case of cold beers, restocking the kitchen refrigerator before returning to bed. This could happen any time during the night or morning and sometimes more than once.

It became so part of my young life that when I was somewhere around the age of eleven or twelve. I decided to open one up for myself while I was downstairs restocking and drink it to help me get back to sleep when I was finished. It wasn't always easy to go back to sleep with all the laughing, shouting, and noise in general from the people having fun in the kitchen, which was the room next to mine. I admit that as I began doing this, I would of course get drunk, resulting in stumbling and problems with speech. But that was never really a problem of getting discovered for a couple of reasons. First, no one paid any attention to me. And if they did, and I made reactions that resembled intoxication it would be attributed to my age, time of day or night, or that they were too drunk themselves to tell, and my being half-asleep—hence the beginning of my drinking at an early age.

My father always thought it would be better to have me doing something related to work than playing. My sisters say that I had it easier than they did, probably because they were so busy inside the house, they didn't notice how busy I was in the cellar or outside. I did all the exterior work, and my sisters did any interior work along with my mother.

I'm writing all of this so that the reader can understand how isolated I typically was from making any close friends with exception of a few in the local area. Two were a year younger than me and one was two years older.

My father always wanted to keep me doing something, anything! We had about a half-acre of land with a section of it (about 50 percent of the half acre) that was lower than the rest and considerably swampy. There were tall weeds throughout standing in swampy water. This area where we lived was generally a high-water table. Just two properties to the east of us was an intersection called Old Tappan Road and Orangeburg Road, which is the street our address was on. On the northeast corner were a couple of acres of swamp that were fairly deep. In the opposite direction, a couple hundred feet down the road was a two-and-a-half-acre sand bottom swimming pool that was hand dug out of a swamp and still water supplied by underground springs that was located on a twenty-acre club grounds. Between them and us was a property that had three hand dug small lakes also fed by underground springs. Those lakes and the swimming pool were where us three kids learned how to skate proficiently, at young ages. In fact, ice skates were the primary gifts that we could expect each year at Christmas. We used to get up at sunrise, evaluate the size and weight of a package and then shake it, to locate and open our skates while our parents were sleeping. Then, the three of us then would go next door, clear any snow off the pond nearest our yard, and skate until they woke up and called us in, hours later.

Now I mentioned the swamp because my father being a contractor had a small bulldozer and backhoe and dump truck. He would bring home trucks full of excavated soils that had debris of tree stumps, branches and rocks it, and dump it in the swamp area. Then it was my job to spread it out with a shovel and rake out the rocks and debris. Throwing them into areas that were not yet filled in. Later, more truckloads were dumped on top of the area that I had just spread and raked out. Then the process was continued again and again until the entire half an acre was brought up to the elevation that the house property was on. I asked my father why I had to spread and rake out the previous load since he was only going to top it off with another load of unfiltered dirt. He told me it was for practice. Bottom line, it was so that I couldn't really have time to spend with friends. That area was finally filled in and raked out so fine that grass was planted. It was also my job to mow the lawn and pick up the cut grass on the property.

My father would at times come home and find me playing catch with my closest friend Ricky in the yard. He'd then tell me to mow the lawn starting in the rear yard because he was then in the front yard, while he would play catch with Ricky. When I finished, he would go inside, and I literally never had a game of catch with him in my life, only watched him play with at times my older sister or one of my three friends. It was my oldest sister who taught me how to play baseball, football, and basketball at my neighbor's garage hoop. Besides those jobs, if there was any time available after school, he would dig holes in the rear or side yard with his backhoe to bury debris that came in from job sites and have me fill in the holes by hand and rake out the rocks to plant grass again.

At the age of about seven, I started being a business owner whenever I had free time. From spring through the fall, I mowed lawns, cleaned out weeds in gardens, and raked up cut grass for neighbors or anyone within a three-mile radius that I could get the work from to make my own money. My majority of customers were in a development called Dearborn estates. I had one property in particular that was owned by a man who was a radio talk show host on local radio channel who often told me how great a job I did for him. He hired me for everything possible around his place, including cleaning out the gutters and some painting. I still remember him giving me verbal praises for my work. He even went as far as telling his audience what a good worker he had using my name. I never got affirmations at home for anything. My father rarely called me by name in fact. I was bonehead, knot head, nitwit, and occasional moron—oh and a few curse words as his terms of endearment.

During the fall, I raked leaves, and in the winter, I'd do snow removal not only on our own property but at neighbors again within that three-mile circle that would hire me. Around that age, my uncle Wick showed us kids how to go into the woods between Thanksgiving and Christmas. We would locate patches of ground ferns, and after removing the snow from the area, I would pick the ferns and put them into neatly stacked packs and place them into paper bags to bring them into the cellar to make Christmas wreaths. Each bunch would then be tied tight with twine and then tied to wire hangers formed into different sized rings to make the wreaths. We put spray snow on them, a plastic red bow, and small pinecones that we also picked from trees in the woods. I would then go house to house getting orders for Christmas. After making each wreath, I'd deliver them to the customers. Christmas wreaths were the biggest moneymaker for me, along with snow removal, so I could purchase presents for my sisters, parents, and family members in the area.

Secrecy

It was the beginning of a very personal secrecy of my life from that time. I had learned not only the importance of keeping my mouth shut, but also the fact that I could do so and live a life of secrecy concerning my own life, as a boy and as a man.

Cellar Secrecy

Like a lot of kids at a young age, I apparently was afraid of the dark. The big mistake was letting my father know! He always had his own way of dealing with situations like this, especially with his son. As I had referred to before, he was, for some reason, ashamed or dissatisfied with me as his son. So he found his ways to try and strengthen my resolve toward making me a better son, one that he may one day be proud of, which never happened. And there were lots of reasons to be proud of me later in my life.

I think that one problem was that my oldest sister (four years older) was a total jock. She could kick a football in her bare feet further than the kicker did at high school football games. So being younger was not included in the assessment of my abilities compared to hers. My other sister was a straight-A student all her life. She went to college and also got her masters. Being called dumb all my young life made me think that I couldn't do good in school, so I barely passed. Comparison to both my sisters was not good. The only ability I had then, and still do, is I do very well in taking tests. Don't ask me why; I have no idea other than I find things in the test to be logical. I never brought books home and still passed the tests somehow.

Consequently, how he decided to cure me of this embarrassing "afraid of the dark" issue at the age of about seven was to make me stay in our cellar, with the lights turned out all night. He knew that my mother would not approve of this method. So I was told to "not only not complain or certainly not to cry," but also not to tell my mother or sisters. This was an issue that was totally between me and him, and I was to be a man and show him that I could take it like one.

It was on an evening when my sisters were staying at someone's house, and it would be just the three of us. After my mother was asleep, he came into our bedroom. I was already awake because he had told me of his decision to do this earlier in the day along with the warnings. He had me come with him to the cellar stairs, told me to go to the bottom and find a place to sleep on the moldy smelling clothing that was down in the bottom room, and go to sleep while he turned off the lights. Our cellar was unfinished, however sectioned off with one dividing wall creating two sections with a doorway between. The stairwell section was the one where he intended to one day finish and the other was where the furnace, water heater, work bench, myriad of tools, building materials, and a sump pump to remove the continual water invasion of the basement were located. Well, I was very familiar with the cellar because it was one of my jobs to clean it up whenever there was flooding, I would remove the floodwaters by carrying the pail with water, up the stairs to the kitchen through the exterior door and dump it outside.

Well, I wasn't really happy or excited about the treatment, but it was partially responsible for my cure of the obsession with the darkness. It wasn't too far into the distance of time that I realized why it was so important for me to be cured of this fear.

My father was doing some work at the swimming pool down the road and I was helping him while he was digging a trench and large hole in the property to put in a water line and storage tank. When we were going home, he told me to get up on the front of the backhoe where the payloader was. I got in the bucket and put my hands alongside me on the top of the bucket to hold on while we were about to go home.

Unknowingly, what would happen, he pulled the lever to raise the bucket off the ground and leaned it back toward the main support arms. Neither he nor I realized that since my hand was on the top of the bucket, my fingers would get squashed between the bucket and the support bar, behind it and at the same height where the bucket top would prevent the bucket from going any further back. Luckily, there must have been a small amount of space between the bucket and the bar, where my fingers were. Because although my fingers got so squeezed that the blood was forced out of the ends of four fingers and fingernails, on each hand, but thankfully no bones were broken.

Of course, I let out a scream, and my father immediately realizing what had occurred, lowered the bucket to release my fingers. What I remember is that although I was only about nine or ten years old, I was told not to cry, and I already wasn't, and didn't. He had Band-Aids in a box under his seat and put a small swab with a tape around it on my fingers and that was that! That's how we were brought up. We were very poor, and doctors were not an option, so deal with it. Oh yeah, and I was an idiot for having my hands there since he apparently thought I was a backhoe designer when I was a kid.

One day, as I was running down our driveway which was covered with mid-sized gravel stone on it, I slipped and fell onto my knees. I was wearing shorts so a sharp-ended gravel about the size of an ice cube went into my knee. I hobbled into the house and told my father who was sitting at the kitchen table. He told me to come to him, and he pulled the rock out of my knee and told me to go and clean it with water and put a Band-Aid on it. The puncture was bleeding profusely as I remember, and a Band-Aid didn't cover the puncture or stop the bleeding. I was able to find a cloth patch to put over it and tape around my leg and knee. After I had done that and walked out into the kitchen, he told me that the lawn needed to be mowed. I still have the scar from that stone in my knee to this day.

The thing is, going to the doctor didn't occur to us. We couldn't and so we didn't think of it when we got hurt. Doctors were not a part of or life because of how poor we were.

I describe all of this only for one reason. I made it through my childhood feeling I was worthless in my father's eyes. But I want the reader to know that it's how you bring up a kid that really determines who they will or may become. I didn't go to college or get good marks in high school because I didn't think of myself as being smart since my father always reminded me that I wasn't. I passed high school while living with my Aunt Marie and Uncle Wick from the age of fourteen. I passed because of my test-taking skills. Later in life I took an IQ test and came up with a high rating. But it's how a person is treated and what they are told that makes or breaks a kid or, should I say, a person.

What I have learned since changing my life is that although my father on earth didn't love me, I have always had a father in heaven that was with me every day of my life. Sadly, I didn't know it! He saved my life so many times. Starting when I was only around five years old and was in a car accident with my mother that not only went off the road and rolled over twice. That was one of numerous instances that should have killed me if not for my Father in heaven looking after me.

More Secrets

When I was about seven years old my mother's brother, Uncle Ed, came out from California to live in New Jersey because he was going through a divorce. He was staying with my grandmother in the house where he grew up in Hillsdale, New Jersey. My Aunt Agnes and Uncle Edwin were also living there, along with my grandmother.

One night he took me to see a movie called the *Ten Commandments*. I remember that I was so impressed and enthralled with that movie that it's still my favorite movie to this very day. I watch it every Easter season after I obtained a VHS of it back in the seventies. I didn't believe in God, so I saw it like a fantasy movie. It isn't!

Anyway, that evening, we returned to my grandmother's house after the movie. We were all talking and discussing the movie in the small kitchen located in the rear of the house, when a knock at the door startled us all because of it being so late. My Uncle Edward answered the door, only to find that there were two policemen there who inquired as to whether my Uncle Eddy was in the house. When they were told he was in the kitchen and were allowed to enter, they told my uncle Ed that he was under arrest for nonpayment of child support. To be fair to him, I remember that before we left for the movie, they were discussing the efforts he had been going through to get a job, ever since he had arrived.

They took him away in handcuffs. We were all shocked at the event and that was the real beginning of my keeping secrets. My grandmother and Aunt Agnes pleaded with me to never tell anyone what had happened. Not even my mother or sisters or anyone because their embarrassment could spread if this got out. I didn't share that experience until they were all deceased, and I was in my sixties and my mother in her mid-eighties. She then exclaimed that she had no idea that it had occurred to that day! I had kept that secret kept until it didn't matter, since I was a seven year old asked to keep it a secret. I did, and "Life goes on."

My First NYC adventures

At the age of twelve, I took on a paper route for the Bergan Evening Record. When I took it over, I had thirty-three customers. When I turned it over and divided into three routes for three kids, I had sold the paper to 155 weekly customers in a little over a year later.

When I was delivering and doing sales for my paper route that year, my dog and best friend, Tag, would run along with me while riding my bike. She knew my customers and knew whether or not she could go up to the door with me or stay by the front of their driveway. Each time I would get a new customer, it didn't take her long to know that they were added and what to do. In the winter in New Jersey, it got very cold and often snowed. During that time, she would choose to stay right beside me 24-7.

My route was not only the largest but also the longest with the Bergen Evening Record, which is why it was divided into three different routes at the time I quit. The paper had certain awards for accomplishments. I received the highest rank ever made in one year due to my increased sales and route size. I think it was called an ACE or HONOR carrier. They had an awards dinner for me and some other older people who worked for the paper. However, I achieved the highest grade or accomplishment and sat at the main table with the owners of the paper. Neither my mother nor father attended the dinner with me to celebrate my accomplishment. The man who delivered the papers to me daily picked me up and brought me to and from the event.

At that dinner, I was awarded two tickets to see the Harlem Globe Trotters at Madison Square Garden in NYC. Again, neither parent would accompany me to the event. So I rode my bike from Old Tappan to Westwood NJ, took a bus to Hackensack, NJ, then another bus that went to NYC, followed by a subway to go to Madison square Garden in midtown New York City by myself. I returned the same way after walking around the city and seeing Forty-Second Street, the bright lights, more people that I had ever been around, buildings so high I couldn't see the tops, and Times Square, which I had seen only on TV for New Year's celebrations. I had to return home at night, on the five-mile ride home by bicycle from Westwood to my friend's house, so that my parents wouldn't know that I had gone by myself. *More secrets!* We didn't tell anyone.

Ricky Rappold was my closest friend growing up, until later in life when I became associated with the mafia and Ricky got married and had children. That is a sad story because after he and his new wife came over for dinner with me and my wife one evening, I never saw him again. Apparently, it was due to me and my life decisions, not anything that he did. I loved him until he died at a young age and still remember him fondly as my closest friend growing up. Ricky's parents owned a twenty-acre daytime resort with a two-acre swimming pool. He and I worked around that place since we were young painting tables, raking leaves, raking beaches, cleaning bathhouses, and eventually life guarding during the summers at the age of fifteen and older. He wasn't like me, in so many ways. The biggest difference was that he was a straight A student in school.

Well, getting back to my NYC episode, I fell in love with NYC! I then convinced Ricky to go with me one weekend during the summer when I was around thirteen and Ricky was around twelve. Ricky was a very handsome kid who also had money, since his parents owned Lake Idlewild later called Fountain Blue. He dressed in his best Nehru-type suit, stylish at that time, and I was in jeans, sneakers, and a short-sleeved shirt. I wanted him to experience New York City, so I took him on my previous route via bikes, buses, and subways. This brought us down to Thirty-Fourth Street near Madison Square Garden. We walked around in awe thinking that we would spend the entire night in the city since we told both our parents that we were each staying at one another's house for the night.

All the bright lights, the crowded streets and sidewalks, the honking horns, masses of people, unbelievably high buildings and stores galore excited us both. We were very happy, until it got late at night and we had roamed somewhere into the west side and down an alley to go to see the Hudson River and the New Jersey lights from the New York side. Not too smart, I know! When we were walking and talking toward the river, we heard what sounded like the snapping of fingers. They probably had seen *West Side Story*. Then we heard two persons snapping their fingers then three, four, and a whole bunch. They started to charge at us but we outran them in speed and didn't stop for at least twenty blocks. We found access to the subway and made our way home. Ricky was much smarter than me. So he "wisely" decided that he would never do that again. As for myself, I found the entire evening to be fun, full of adrenaline, and consequently very exciting. Those were the two real beginnings of my love for the big city lights.

Age of Fourteen

Besides all the issues that have been talked about in my youth with my father, it was just the beginning of a very memorable year.

I had a female dog that I wrote about earlier when I described my paper route, and her name was Tag. She was with me for my entire life up until the spring of 1962, just before I turned fourteen. She was my absolute best friend in my life, and I often give her credit for saving my life because of how she showed her love for me and me for her. I say that because when I was just a young kid, I used to think about ways to kill myself. And as I got older, I thought about suicide way too often. Having her with me before and directly after school she was always there and always full of love, which I needed. We would walk in the woods together, sit together, run after balls that I would throw, and I used to sneak her into the house to sleep with me. My grammar school was about two miles away from where we lived, and she would sometimes get out of her chained collar and come to meet me in the ball field behind the school. She knew that was where we should meet so that she wouldn't get in trouble with the school. I would most often go in that direction after school to a friend's house, or just meet with some of my friends before going home to do my endless chores. Sadly, she was diagnosed with heartworms, which was slowly killing her. Consequently, we had to put her down to give her peace and remove her constant pain. My mother and I rode together to the vet's office where I had to carry her into the vets to be put down by injection. I carried her in knowing that she was going to be killed and I would never have her at my side ever again. What I regret the most is that back then, you had to leave the animals with the vet without being there with them when they went to sleep and never recovered.

It was also the year that I lost my virginity. My two older sisters (two and four years older) taught me how to dance beginning at the age of about four. They used me as a dancing partner, which taught me how to dance the current dances. I remember that I was doing the "HOP" at the age of five at a friend's birthday party. I had become a good dancer. I remember going to school and CYO dances winning dancing contests because of what I had been practicing with my sisters. I also remember from when I was just a kid at the age of sixteen, dancing in nightclubs, and getting served alcohol because I was six feet, five inches tall, around 210 pounds, and looked older. Girls would come up to me and ask me to dance while all the other guys were standing along the walls wanting to do what I was doing because I was always with the girls.

It was just before the end of the school year and I was walking toward home after school, and it was really hot. On the way home, there is a concrete bridge that goes over a stream coming from the woods. I often would go down to the stream and sit by the water, enjoying the coolness and solitude in the woods. This time, when I went down and into the woods, walking for a short while to get to a spot in the stream that I knew had a deeper area. I saw two sisters that I had known for several years. They were naked and sitting in the water because it was a typical New Jersey hot and muggy day. I walked out of the bushes that grew along the riverbank and startled them and myself. I stood there for a few seconds wondering how I should deal with this embarrassment, when one of the sisters said, "Why don't you come in and join us?" Well, yeah! So I stripped and sat sown between them in the stream where it was somewhat deeper. I will admit that the cold water didn't do much good with my manhood. But that was quickly overcome. The next thing that happened is they both started to put their hands on me, which was the beginning of losing my virginity with two older girls, who were sisters, and me at the age of fourteen. However, it wasn't their first time, for sure.

It was a bad year, but that helped me get through it. Please, readers, I am not saying that a boy or girl should lose their virginity at the age of fourteen. I just mean that although I see it as wrong now, it helped me then because of all my other problems, with my father, losing my best friend, Tag, a near-death accident (that is explained next), and running away from home.

Later that year, at the beginning of the summer, I was with my father's friend, Beaky, the beer delivery guy. He had also become a friend of mine. He was a great guy. We were together one day on the Hudson River in his speedboat. We went from Nyack, NY up to where the Second World War battleships were anchored in an area called the "Battleship Graveyard," a long way up the river north of Haverstraw, NY. We went up to the anchored ships sitting in a row, positioned side by side from the riverbank out into the Hudson River. There were several rows of these enormous battle ships used during WWII. They towered over our heads so high that it was (as I remember it) unsettling. We went up and down between the ships just exploring their size and configurations as warships. We pretty much spent the day on the river, and it was getting dark when we pulled out the boat to go home. I remember the day well and the special time that we had together. Time that I never had with my father—ever!

We had dropped off the boat and trailer and were heading home on Highway Route 303, heading south toward New Jersey. I was asleep in the passenger's front seat, without a seat belt on, as they weren't required by law back then. An elderly couple was heading north on Route 303 apparently looking to turn off onto the Garden State Parkway. Both cars were doing at least the speed limit of fifty-five miles per hour or more. Apparently, the couple heading north saw the turn off to the Garden State Highway at the last second, and he turned directly into our lane, which caused a head on crash. It was like hitting a tree at one hundred miles per hour. I don't know or remember what happened to the people in the other car. In fact, I was told what happened to us/me by Beaky while I was in the hospital.

Consequently, I had gone through the windshield and slid across the hood into some weeds on the side of the road (I was later told by Beaky). The police and ambulances came directly to the accident and Beaky was brought to the Nyack hospital in a daze with minor wounds himself. After a short time, he asked how I was, and he was told that he was the only one that was in his car. He went crazy telling the doctors, nurses, and police that I had been with him! He demanded they go and look for me.

The police at the hospital contacted the police still at the scene of the accident and told them that they were told by the driver of car that was heading south, there was someone else who was in the car. The cars were being hitched up to tow truck flat beds, and I was lying in the high grass on the side of the road, unconscious. The police found me, and I was immediately also sent to the hospital, where I was still unconscious until the next day or more.

One of the reasons why I even mention this is because I had just graduated from grammar school and was going to high school in the fall. Only now I had shaved areas in my head and lots of stitches. My skin had been peeled back along the top of my skull and along my forehead. Great way to start your high school days! Especially for a kid that has been told all his short life that he was worthless and had just lost his best friend, his beloved dog, Tag. Luckily, my hair was fairly long because Elvis was my star in life. I had a haircut like his that could be combed over the scares pretty good, with exception of a large still red scare on my forehead which is visible to this day. I of course wore a hat as much as I could, but in those days, you couldn't wear a hat in school. In fact, you could get suspended if your hair went over the collar of your shirt.

Another contributing factor to the drama of my fourteenth year was my own fault. There was a new kid that came to our school in the eighth grade and I didn't treat him very good. I don't know why but I kind of bullied him with challenges not physical force, which made him mad at me. He was actually a nice kid. I think it was in the first month of high school, and I was on my way home when he and a friend of his approached me on the ball field. They ganged up on me, and I wound up on the ground looking up at them. This was a very upsetting position for me. I was warned not to get up or else risk being decked by the two of them. I didn't know what would happen if I got in a fight, whether or not my scars that were still pretty new might open up. So they just called me a couple of names, one of them "scarred," and I just sat there and took it.

However, it was a lesson in two ways. The first was, shame on me for bullying that kid in the first place. I had never done that before. The second was, I'd never stay on the ground again, no matter what!

It was sometime later that I decided to run away from my father. I truly loved New York City and knew that I could hide there from anyone, including the police.

Runaway Kid

When I had had enough of my father's abuse, I decided to leave home. I had an argument with my father and told him I was going to my aunt and uncles to stay with them. I had been talking about doing that for a few months and my parents assumed that I had then gone to be with them for a while. I was somewhat familiar with the area around Madison Square Garden and Times Square in New York City. I thought that I could get away to that neighborhood and hide out from being brought back home again. I really wanted to get away from him and his obvious dislike and abuse. Not physically, but constantly, emotionally. That could be another book!

I road my bike to Westwood which was about five miles from our house in Old Tappan. I stopped about a half mile before getting there and hid my bike in a small wooded area with lots of high strong bushes before walking the rest of the way to catch a bus to Hackensack. I then took one of the buses that I had taken before when I went to see the Globe Trotters by myself, and again when I went with my best friend "Ricky." The bus stops went over the George Washington Bridge, so you can go to the subway system and down to the Madison Square Garden, and Hell's Kitchen area.

When I arrived at the stop and came up the stairs from the subway, I remember that I was scared. I had no idea where I was going to go to, where I was going to sleep, eat, or be safe. I walked along Broadway up to Forty-Second Street and saw hundreds of people of all ages, all colors, and knew no one. I walked around all night long wondering where I should go, and how I'd survive. I had some money that I had saved doing all kinds of work in the neighborhood back home. But didn't want to spend any, thinking that I needed to save it to eat when necessary. I bought a slice of pizza and a Coke and savored that as if it was my last meal. Through it all, I never once considered going back home. I felt free, not being near my father.

I walked around all night when finally, a policeman stopped me and said he had been watching me for hours and wanted to know why I was roaming the street and not at home. I told him that I was upset and was just going to return home. He asked me where I lived, and I told him down on Thirty-Sixth Street and Tenth. I must have lucked out because I had no idea where that was, or if there was a building there that housed people. I started walking south on Broadway toward Thirty-Sixth after he let me go.

I continued walking south and saw where there was a fifty-gallon drum alongside a building that had a fire going in it. It was really cold, so I went over to it and was standing there warming my hands and my body when a man came out of the shadows and walked up on the opposite side of the barrel. He didn't' say anything until after he had warmed up a little and asked me why I was out so late. I didn't have an answer, so I just kept my head down and continued to warm my hands. He then said that he knew that I must have run away from home because of the look on my face. He said it was a look of anger, determination, confusion, and some fear. He then continued talking to me about what to look for in order to keep myself safe. He told me that I had to be really tough with the kids in the neighborhood because they would definitely challenge me. And to keep away from anyone who was drunk or looked like he was high on drugs. The thing about that was, I had no idea what he was talking about because there were no drugs in the small town that I had just come from, with exception of some newly discovered marijuana. And that was sparse because I had only heard of it, never knew anyone who was doing it. It was 1962 and things were just starting to get going in the field of drugs in our little town of Old Tappan, New Jersey.

He then showed me a building that he said I would be okay to sleep in for the night, because I could lock the door in one of the rooms and there was a window where I could escape should I need to. I had to trust someone, and he appeared like he was an honest man. Of course, I also had a good sized pocket knife if needed, which probably wouldn't have helped anyway. Some other men walked up and he introduced me as a friend, which apparently gave me some protection because no one was rude or nasty to me. I eventually went into the building that he had suggested, locked the door to the room, curled up against a wall with a piece of wood and my knife in my hands for protection, and went to sleep. The building was abandoned except for the rats, and there was no heat, so it was really cold. Not only because of the weather, but because of the atmosphere of my mind and heart.

I remember how I felt sitting against the wall in that apartment, frightened, angry, and missing my mother and my best friend, Tag.

The next morning, I woke up at the first light and went outside, I saw that man sitting next to my door covered in blankets. He got up and we walked together to a small hole in the wall where we were able to get a cup of hot coffee and a roll to eat. He asked if I had any blankets to keep warm at night. I said no, and he brought me to a used everything store where I purchased two blankets and a really old and cheap backpack to put the blankets in and keep with me, so they wouldn't get stolen. He continued to be a friend to me for weeks and introduced me to a few of the local kids in the area. All the kids were like me. They had no place to go or didn't want to return to where they had come from.

The kids had formed a gang by the name of the "Park Rats." That was because they spent much of their time in a small park located just outside of the Lincoln tunnel. At first it was okay. But then one of the guys who was supposedly the gang leader challenged me by pushing me onto ground and telling me that if I got up, he was going to give me a beating. I don't remember what started him off, but I wasn't about to just sit there on the ground and let him try and intimidate me in front of the others. I knew immediately that that would be the wrong decision. I started to get up and he tried to kick me, which was way too obvious. I caught his leg, twisted it, and put him on the ground while I stood up. I let him get up (which was stupid, as I later learned, because the reason why you put someone on the ground is to kick him, while he is on the ground) and waited for him to rush me. And he did! We were about the same size, but I was stronger because of all the work I had had to do with my father over my short years, I was able to throw him onto the ground again. I could see that he was really upset about that, and I just stood back and waited again for his move. He got up as fast as he could and ran toward me swinging. I blocked off most of his punches and got in a lucky hard haymaker that nearly broke his jaw and put him down again. I then said that I didn't know why he was so mad at me and that we should just cool it. He put his hand out and said…because we needed to know if you would fight or run, and, if you were any good at fighting. I explained that I was taught how to fight by a friend of mine called Michael M who used to kick my butt constantly throughout grammar school. They laughed, and we shook hands and continued to be friends.

Those were the days when gangs fought other gangs. Just like in the *West Side Story*. If you have never seen that movie, get it. If we saw someone stealing a pocketbook from a woman, we would run him down, beat the crap out of him, and return the pocketbook to the woman it was stollen from, contents intact. Sometimes we got a tip for our honesty and service. Just because we were on the streets away from our homes, didn't mean that we had no morals. Doing anything to a girl or woman was unacceptable to me because of my love for my two sisters and my mother.

It got around that there was a new kid on the block, and I often had to defend myself in a fight against some kid that thought that he could beat me. All I can say is, I'm glad that Michael was not in the neighborhood. Or if he was, I'd hope that we were still friends. Anyway, I did very well and built a reputation of being a good fighter and a good guy, who didn't pick on anyone and only defended myself.

We had a fight against another gang, kind of like the *West Side Story*. Oh, wait a minute, it was a "west side story" on the west side of Manhattan, where we were, in Hell's Kitchen, 1962.

Well, I spent all my money and no one else had any either so we were sitting around deciding what we should do. Sleeping in an abandoned unheated building was bad enough, but no food was not good. One of the boys named Jimmy told us that his older brother used to steal cars and sell them to a chop shop up in Yonkers, NY. He said that he made good money for the effort and suggested that we do the same. I said steal, not hijack, like these punks do today. The problem was that no one knew how to jump a car except me.

My Uncle Wick was a carpenter by trade and a natural mechanic also. He and my Aunt Rie were the ones who had no children and treated me and my sisters like we were theirs. My uncle made me a go-kart that had a 7.5 horsepower Briggs & Stratton gas motor in it. With a hand clutch, gas pedal, brakes, and a plywood skin over a steel chassis that made it look like a three-fourths midget racer. He kept it at their home a couple of cities away from my home in Old Tappan, NJ, but I learned to ride and repair it efficiently for years.

I not only learned how to fix everything on that go-kart, but how to fix things on a car engine. He had showed me several times how to jump start a car engine, only in case I needed to do it in the future when I started driving. Hence, I knew how to jump-start an engine. I also knew how to drive a car, a truck, a backhoe, and a bulldozer because my father owned all of them.

We made an arrangement that I would jump-start a parked car and Jimmy who was going on seventeen would drive it to where his brother used to sell them. We did get a new car jumped and he went to a chop shop that his older brother told him about in Yonkers New York, and got $400 cash for the car. We lived off that for a while and then decided to steal another.

That heist turned out to be a bad move because we got caught in the process of my being under the hood and Jimmy sitting at the wheel when two policemen who were walking around the corner spotted us. They asked us what we were doing, and we said it was Jimmy's car and it wouldn't start. Then we were asked for his license and the registration for the car. We were arrested and taken to a police station where we were questioned about our age where we lived and where our parents were. We both refused to tell them so they told us we would have to be put in jail for the night and put in a type of orphanage until they could contact our parents because of our age.

I didn't like those options of being held anywhere especially an orphanage and decided to tell them where I was from and what the phone number was to call my parents. When they called my father answered the phone because my mother wasn't at home at that time. He got the address for the police station and came to pick me up.

We were not being arrested because we had not actually started or taken the car, and we were so young, so they let us go with our parents. When I was released to my father, he assured the police that they would never see me again. On the way home he of course was yelling at me as usual and telling me what a jerk I was. He said that my mother didn't know, and he didn't want her to know that he had to come to NYC to pick me up from a police station because I was caught trying to steal a car. When he finally became quiet, I told him that I ran away to get away from him and his verbal abuse, calling me names like stupid, moron, idiot, nitwit, dumb and a myriad of others. I told him that as soon as I could I was going to run away again, and the only way to prevent that would be to tie me up. He then told me that if I really wanted to leave home that I was to promise him that I would finish my high school education and graduate. I asked him why he cared if I got an education since all he did was tell me how stupid I was. He said because my mother is going to be very upset that I have decided to leave and stay with my aunt and uncle. She would be really upset to think that I would quit school and not get an education. He also said that I wasn't ever to ask for any money because I had to support myself if I left. I responded that that would be fine with me. And kept my word!

I talked with my Uncle Wick and Aunt Marie and asked them if I could be allowed to live with them. They both agreed and I lived with them and never went home to live with my father again. We saw one another on holidays and family get-togethers, but I never had to live with him again. My aunt and uncle were wonderful. I had to keep my room clean and bed made first thing in the morning. (I still do that.) I had to do my own laundry walking about one and a half miles one way to a laundromat. I often made some of my own meals or helped with my aunt cooking and always helped clean up. I helped around the house by vacuuming, polishing the wood floors, dusting, and doing outside chores like mowing the lawn, washing the cars, and straightening up Uncle Wick's toolshed.

That was nothing like I used to do when living with my father who always found work for me either at home or cleaning up a job site.

My Aunt Marie went with me to school and spoke with the principal while I waited in the outer office. I have no idea what she said to him, but when they came out of the principal's office, my aunt gave me a kiss and said goodbye. The principal told me to go into his office with him. He closed the door and gave me the expected scolding, along with some strict directions about having to be able to study hard in order to bring myself back to where my courses were. I was going to speak with my different teachers and see to it that I did exactly that.

I had few friends when I was growing up because I was always at home or at one of my father's jobs working. I joined the cub scouts when I was about six and had to quit because we couldn't afford a uniform. I couldn't join the Little League due to the same reason. Bottom line is we were the poorest family in town, but my father always had money to drink at bars, have friends over for drinking parties, and have his extramarital affairs.

Here's the thing about my relationship with my father. As explained above he never gave me any credit for anything even when I had correctly completed jobs that he had given me. And of course, when I became associated with a crime family, he really didn't say anything positive. But as you will read later, I finally was able to get out of the criminal activities and move to San Diego, California. Within six months, I was a foreman on a construction of a bank. Construction plans were and are very simple for me to understand and evaluate. And being a manager of two trucking companies in charge of many drivers gave me an ability to manage hundreds of men over the years. So within a year, I was a commercial construction superintendent. I built a total of four banks, two shopping malls, an opera house, several subterranean parking structures, a seven-story office building, and several other commercial projects. I then moved to Lake Tahoe, California, and designed and constructed custom homes.

I mentioned this for two reasons. The first is my father never even said "well done" or "wow." I had no idea you could do these things. Nothing—ever! The second reason is to tell kids or even adults that just because you don't have a college education doesn't mean you are worthless, or beneath anyone else, or that you can't achieve what you put your mind, heart, and attitude toward. Everyone can make it if you believe in yourself and work hard toward it.

When I lived with my aunt and uncle, I had a job after school at a wood cabinet shop located in another town (Norwood) about one and half miles away from school. Then I walked home to river Vale (my aunt and uncle's house) about three miles from the wood shop. However, I was always hitchhiking and often got rides in those days.

I used to go back to NYC on weekends so that I could and be with my Park Rat friends. I grew to love the city and went there often, by myself and with friends from high school who drove!

When I was about sixteen years old, I could get served alcohol without even being asked for identification because of my size and demeanor. I was in NYC visiting my friends (the Park Rats) when we decided to steal another car because they needed money for food and general existence. This time I not only jumped the car but drove it to Yonkers, NY, where it would be brought to a chop shop for cash. On the way, to my horror, I was pulled over by a New York State Trooper for speeding. I immediately considered getting out of the car, knocking out the cop and fleeing the scene.

However, let me tell everyone who reads this: New York State troopers are like Marines or any of the elite services that protect America. They are big, in perfect shape, heavenly trained and real scary when I faced him. I'm six feet, five inches, and he not only was taller but looked like Arnold Schwarzenegger.

So I quickly decided that that plan wouldn't work. He asked for my license and registration as expected and said they were in the glove compartment of the car. I went to the car and opened the glove compartment acting like I was looking for my license and registration to the car, which I had stolen.

He was standing outside the driver's door and asked, "Why do you look so nervous, kid?" I said I must have left my license and the registration at home when I left the house in such a hurry. He said, "Why are you in a hurry?" I told him that I received a call from my mother who was with my grandmother at the hospital in Yonkers because she thinks that my grandmother may have had a heart attack. He then said, "Okay, kid, go ahead to the hospital and be with your family, but don't drive beyond the speed limit it's dangerous for you and possibly for other drivers." I told him I would and thanked him for letting me go.

Back then, they had radios but no computers. When he got back to the police station and saw that the car had been stolen. I'll bet he flipped out and probably looked for me for years.

When I graduated high school, I got a job with a commercial construction company that was building a large one-story steel building. I became good at concrete forms and all kinds of carpentry and masonry. So they had me help the foreman one evening working overtime. The concrete slab was poured in sections with heavy Visqueen plastic hanging from the steel joists around the perimeter of the poured slab. Then a gas salamander (heater) was put inside the Visqueen area on the slab to keep the slab warm all night so it would cure correctly. The salamander had to be watched all night in order to change the gas tanks when it went out of gas. I was going to stay all night for that reason. My foreman was putting up the two-by-four wood runners on the steel joists, so that the plastic could be nailed to it making a surrounding perimeter of plastic to keep the hot air in. But he was a mason! He knew concrete but he sucked at hammering nails. He was about fourteen or fifteen feet in the air standing on an extension ladder, with one arm through the area between the top runners holding the nails in place, and the other arm trying to nail it into the wood. It was obvious that he was nervous or better yet scared of falling off that ladder, which is why he had his one arm through the top rung area to keep him steady.

He kept on bending the nails and cursing continually because of his frustration and fear. I was at the foot of the extension ladder getting whatever he needed, laughing about his inability to drive in his nails. Knowing me, probably teasing him while laughing. I asked him if he wanted me to take over the task because I knew how to hammer nails. I asked this as a recommendation to help. He threw the hammer at me from at the top of the ladder. I instinctively moved and it just missed hitting me. Then he said get the hammer and give it to me and I'll come down to where I could reach and take it from you. The problem was I was already picking up the hammer and then walking back to the bottom of the ladder.

When I got to the ladder, I hooked the claw of the hammer onto the bottom rung of the ladder and pulled the ladder out from under him. He fell and because he still had his arm hooked in between the two rungs, he fell on it, breaking it. While he was on the ground screaming at me. I calmly walked over to where he was, bent over, and punched him in the face, saying "I quit, and you're lucky that that hammer didn't hit me! If it had, I'd have hit you in the head with it instead of punching you. And if you try to press charges against me. I will be getting you arrested for throwing the hammer at me, you dumb bastard."

I left him there on the ground with a broken arm still under the ladder that had him pinned to the ground. We didn't have cell phones back then, and there wasn't anyone else on the job site. Too bad! I left and got another job as a carpenter in Orangeburg, New York, and they appreciated my work and carpenter abilities.

THE BEGINNING

Anthony's Request

> "And if it is disagreeable in your sight to
> serve the LORD, choose for yourselves
> today whom you will serve: whether the
> gods which your fathers served which were
> beyond the River, or the gods of the Amorites
> in whose land you are living; but as for me
> and my house, we will serve the LORD."
> —Joshua 24:15 (NAS)

Joshua...what a man of God and of valor. He did choose to follow God and he will be remembered by man and God forever. I originally took to following Satan and the world instead of our Lord. However, I didn't know that there was really another way. That's probably not true. I knew that I shouldn't have taken the road to sin and crime, but I didn't believe that there was any other way for a person like me to achieve life's desires without the help of or connection to crime. And I was a pure atheist because of my father. I never prayed, thought of God, or thought that there was a god. When I was given the opportunity, however shady it may be, I took it!

My introduction to the real criminal world started because I had just lost a job as a carpenter. I was married by now, with a kid on the way. When my wife went into labor I needed to bring my wife to the hospital to deliver our first child instead of going to work. She went into labor around six o'clock in the morning. At that time, I had no way to contact the men I was working with to let them know that I wouldn't be able to go to work, since there were no cell phones in 1968. Also, my boss had no secretary or any way of contacting him, to let him know I wouldn't be there.

When I did go to work the next day (with a lot of pride and a few cigars that bragged "It's a boy") my boss fired me. My boss said in no uncertain terms (and with a lot of expletives) that he had six kids and never lost a day at work because of them. Well, I believe he was being truthful, as we did NOT share the same view of fatherhood obviously. He declared that I was fired because I hadn't gone to work instead of bringing and being with my wife at the hospital. There were a few other words to the conversation that became an altercation and that's when he decided to scream in my face and tell me to "get out of here" before pushing me. Bad move, because that's when I hit him with a roundhouse to his jaw that he never imagined I would throw, knocking him down. I started to walk away when he jumped up and took a swing at me. He was big and strong, but also slow and stupid, so I commenced to give him a total whooping, with a whole lot of anger.

The other man on the job, older than me but younger than the boss, came running over and got between us, stopping me beating him up. Back in those days, when men got into a fight nobody called the cops. We just either won or lost. Especially in the construction field. I know he had no idea that he would have lost to me, since I was nineteen years old and he outweighed me by thirty to forty pounds of muscle. However, the problem became that word got around fast in the construction industry. Because construction men usually meet at the same bars in the same areas. And the word that got out wasn't in my favor. Consequently, it was difficult to get a job in the construction field anywhere in that area. Of course, I never shared this event with my wife. She was home with a newborn child and didn't need any more stress because of my reactions to this mutt.

I spent several days looking for work and then it became evident that I was unemployed, and the issue got back to my father-in-law, who incidentally hated my guts with a passion. In fact, I learned a few years later that he attempted to have me killed, but that's in another chapter.

Anthony (my father-in-law) still hated me for getting his daughter pregnant. Can you imagine that? So I get a call from him one day telling me to meet him at his home in Closter, New Jersey.

I reluctantly went there, and he informed me that there may be some work for me. With the words "If you're man enough to get it." Automatically knowing how he feels about me, I realize this is *not going to be a "come on over and play with me" type of job.* He explains that there is a trucking company located in downtown NYC called Breen Airfreight, which is having union problems with their workers and drivers and is currently under a pretty nasty strike. Consequently, Breen is hiring men for laborers, helpers, dockworkers, and drivers for their airfreight PU&D (pickup and delivery) services.

He continues to explain to me that the hourly pay is exceptional for two reasons. First, they need men, and second, but not unimportant, is that I must go through picket lines set up by some pretty aggravated teamsters to do the work. After explaining this to me he gives me his whimsical smile like… "Do you have the balls, ya little mutt?"

It took me about ten seconds to ask, "What's the address?"

He laughed out loud and said, "I gotta give you this much, kid, you may have a set o' balls on you. After all, we'll see." Then he tells me to sit down so we can have an understanding.

He informed me that I need to go to the Breen office in the morning (which includes going through the picket line) and see the owner, Matthew Breen. I'm to let him know that Anthony sent me and see if he still has work that he can use me for. But the top priority for Anthony is not to mention any of this to his daughter, my wife. If I get the job, I can't let my wife Ellen know that there is a strike because it will continue to be dangerous or at least possibly unhealthy until the strike is over. He asks me if he can trust me to keep this quiet, or in other terms "keep your mouth shut." I tell him that although I realize who he is, besides being my father-in-law, I keep secrets better than anyone he knows, and then I left. We went our separate ways. I know he was watching me leave, hoping that I would get shot on the first day, and he could genuinely claim that he had no hand in it. I had already been looking for work on every street in Bergenfield, New Jersey, and surrounding cities. This would just be a place I stumbled on and showed up for.

Well, the next morning, I left our apartment in Bergenfield, New Jersey, around 5:00 a.m. so that I could hopefully be at the trucking company (in downtown NYC) no later than six thirty. My wife knew that I was looking for work and that I would be gone all day. The scary part of this is that there had been several shootings throughout the area due to the Black Panthers being on the war path at that time. Our first apartment was located above a liquor store on the main street of Bergenfield, New Jersey.

Well, I got there at six fifteen and there were about ten or more teamsters standing in the street, trying to look tough. I put my mind to thinking that they were yacking like a bunch of old women. I started to walk toward Breen Airfreight trucking building or in trucking terms known as their "barn." As I approached the picket line a few of the men walked forward while a few others gathered around me and asked me where I was going. I told them I was going into the Breen building. Then they asked me what I was going there for. I told them that actually, I didn't believe it was any of their f———ing business where I was going or for what reason. With that, they all pretty much snickered and moved in closer to try and intimidate me. I already had decided on how I was going to handle this situation, so I just kept calm and waited for my opening. The shop steward, who considered himself a real terror, told me that if I was going into Breen's to look for work, which meant I was willing to cross their picket line, then I had better think more than twice about that. I asked him why. He and a few others jumped in by yelling out, "Because if you try, we will beat the shit out of you!"

Well, that was the information that I had wanted to obtain so I calmly backed out of the crowd, turned around, and headed for my vehicle. All the while hearing a bunch of comments as to what kind of pussy, scared, frightened punk kid I was (being only twenty years old). There was laughter and comments about how I thought I was going to break their picket line.

Well, when I returned to my vehicle of which, I had enough street smarts to know to be parked far enough away from where they couldn't see which one mine was. I took out my Louisville slugger baseball bat, locked the doors, and walked back toward the picket line around the corner. When they saw me…suddenly there was a silence from the mighty men who thought I was a yellow punk, pussy, chicken. And I believe I thought I saw several of the teamsters lay an egg because they sure looked pretty sickly and yellow seeing me (six feet, five inches tall, in great shape, and an obvious attitude to win) walking toward them with a baseball bat in my hand. However, they did rise up for the occasion as I approached. I got to within about two yards from them, and I informed them that I was going into Breen's, and if they had anything to say or do about it, then let it be done or move out of my way.

About four or five of them made a mad rush for me but their hearts were not truly "in it"—at least not as much as mine was. After I took a few or more hits to all parts of my body, including my head, and had batted a few of them down. I was on my way and on the inside of the picket line heading toward the office, with a lot of talking, and yelling going on behind me. I know you're thinking how did I came out on top against four or five men. Attitude! They were on strike and knew that someday the strike will be over. Me? I just had a kid and already had to beat the snot out of a guy because I had a kid. Attitude, never back up no matter what. You can't win by running away! They knew they couldn't follow me onto Breen's property. Plus, there were already non-union and/or management men there that had driven through the line with their trucks just itching for them to follow me onto the Breen property.

As it was Matthew Breen had been standing on the dock observing the entire incident. As I approached, he called out with a rather big smile on his face, "Nice work, and what exactly can I do for you?" He knew exactly what I wanted, but he wanted to be sure that he was totally in control, and that I knew it. Not to mention that my father-in-law told him that I was getting the job, period.

I believe that was the only time I saw that man with a smile. We went into his office and after a short interview I was hired as a trucking helper until I got to know the city and some routes, in order to advance to a driver.

That day, my job consisted of sorting freight and loading trucks until quitting time, which was about 6:00 p.m. that evening. Then

I had to go home to New Jersey on the west side highway to go over the George Washington Bridge and side roads to Bergenfield, which took about ninety minutes. However, leaving work was not a problem, as there were no picket lines at the end of the day. They were probably all in bars, giving their recollection of what happened with a tall very determined kid, and how they taught me a lesson by kicking my butt.

When I got home, I told my wife Ellen that I had a job and she was understandably ecstatic since we were broke and had a new baby. A few scratches, a few bruises, and a shower and nothing was discussed as to any danger or problems with the new job. So that was the beginning of secrecy with my father-in-law. If my ex-wife reads this book, it will probably be the first time she even hears about the truth with this job. She, of course, knew later that he had sent me to Breen for the job, but not about the picket line and my actions.

The next day, I encountered similar confrontations with the picket line. They appeared to me to be different men, with exception of the shop steward. I do believe that they had definitely heard of me. My saving grace was my determination, attitude, and of course fighting and batting abilities. This time was nowhere as bad as the first encounter. I used the bat as a jabbing weapon and put them out of my way. I made it through and started another day with some respect not only from them, but from the men who were working on the dock, because they had all seen the action on both days. After that second day, all I received was verbal abuse from a lot of entitled picket men, understanding that their efforts would be useless and possibly painful if they tried to prevent my entry for work. My family was definitely more important than theirs, in my mind; thus, I was going to work, and they weren't going to stop me. If they brought more men to gang up on me, I probably would have gone back to my car for my crow bar AND my tire iron.

After a few weeks, I was given my own truck with a helper. I had drawn a route through the fur district since Breen believed I could handle myself under situations that may necessitate not only brawn but brains. He apparently believed I had both along with fearless-ness, and some ability to prevail under unusual circumstances, and the fur route needed all of it. The fur route typically had pallets of raw hides, which smelled like nothing I had ever smelled before or since. However, the hides were valuable. There were also large standing boxes that had mink and other valuable coats in them that were delivered to different stores for sales.

That wasn't the last of the picketers' attempts to defer me from working at Breen. After I became a truck driver, my windshield was once shot out, and later one of my tires blew out while on a highway heading out to the Kennedy airport. When I got back to the trucking barn, the mechanic looked at the tire and told me that he believed that it had been shot. I also believe that whoever did that was educated by friends of Anthony's that it was wrong, and there would be severe consequences if it ever happened again mainly because of his association with Breen trucking. I believe that Anthony and his friends must have seen to it that the picketers backed off from me. After their apparent education there was never another problem.

I was given a helper who was called "The Boston Stomper" (or something like that). He was in his mid-forties and had been a fairly successful boxer up in Boston until he lost too many fights because he had broken his hands that kept him out of the ring. I would pick him up a few blocks from the barn and we then went directly to a liquor store where he purchased a "gallon" of cheap wine to help him through the day. I could care less! He worked hard and when I needed him to hold a parking spot for me...he always did it with a smile, for me and a fist for anyone who challenged him.

When you're doing deliveries in NYC, especially downtown, it's really hard to get a parking spot near where you're delivering your freight. I was delivering raw furs on pallets. They had to be taken off the truck with a handlift and lowered onto the ground with an electric tailgate. Then, they were brought into the building's lobby, onto the elevator and into the offices or storerooms. As I tried to describe, the raw furs smelt like a dead animal, figure that! A four-by-four-by-four-foot pile of dead animal furs. And a truck full of them. Ugh.

Well, when you see a parking spot either empty or about to be empty you send out your helper to stand in the parking spot until you can get into it. The problem was (way too often) that you may have to drive around the block before getting to the parking spot that you spotted from a distance. That's where my Boston Stomper came in handy. Because he always kept the spot, even when some other helper or driver thought that they would force him to leave it to them. He enjoyed those moments.

One day the dispatcher for Breen asked me if I could do them a favor. He said that the driver who was to take a semi-truckload to a Queens address was sick and they needed to get the load of freight there. I had practiced with backing in semis at the Breen barn whenever I could. And wanted to get a commercial driver's license (CDL) in the hope that I could get transferred to local semi trips. I agreed and took the load to a warehouse located in Queens. However, on my way, I came to a corner that I had to make a sharp turn to the right in order to continue. But there was a small compact convertible car, a MG or the like, parked illegally on the corner. I honked several times, but no one came to the car, so I tried to get around the corner with it there. I came close but wasn't able to get around the car parked illegally, preventing me to get around the corner. Cars were backed up behind me honking like crazy and people were coming out of buildings to see what all the commotion was about. I got out of the truck to see just how close I was to the car and saw that the rear wheels of the trailer couldn't get around the car. Horns honking and people yelling for me to get out of the way. I went back into the cab and put the transmission in low/low.

I then popped the clutch and increased the gas. The rear wheels of the trailer dragged the car about five feet and then rolled up over the trunk, into and out of the driver's compartment, over the front hood and slammed down on the pavement. The car was a total complete wreck. People were cheering and laughing, and I went on to my destination. I never heard a word about that incident. People in NYC areas mind their own business, and no one called the police or told them my license plate number. When that jerk who owned that car finally went to his car, he must have fainted. What was he going to tell his insurance company or the police? He was parked illegally, and it looked like an airplane hit it and flew off.

I worked for Breen for several months and then the union strike was settled. That, unfortunately, meant I was then out of a job as a driver. The Teamsters were not going to allow me to join when I was a strike breaker. Breen liked me, so he moved me into the office as an assistant dispatcher. I was doing that for a short while. Until I was sent up to another trucking company in Rye New York as a "new" driver for that barn.

I went up to Rye in Westchester County to a trucking outfit called Dion Delivery service. It had about ten trucks at that time and were doing all of Emery Air Freights pickup and delivery services throughout Westchester County, NY; Fairfield County, Connecticut; and Orange County, NY. This place was at a stalemate I found out later, since the dispatcher was also a union man. The terminal manager was an Emery Air Freight man who had no idea how to manage not only a barn, but drivers or a dispatcher. He was just a Rat who reported to Emery his opinion of the actions of the barn, whose trucking company was Dion Delivery Service.

I was given all the routes to learn. I just thought that it was in case the route needed to be filled in due to a sickness or vacation or any other reason. I learned them all! And did them well, in fact, eventually better than the other drivers because they were union and I was not. The other drivers were thinking that I was a new driver waiting to be inducted into the Teamsters Union. I really wasn't aware of what was going on, but I knew that I couldn't be a union driver, because of my actions at Breen.

Then I was told that the owner of Dion Delivery, a man maned Vincent, had fired the dispatcher, and I was to take his place. Needless to say, the drivers didn't like me, especially since they thought that I knew what was going to happen. However, I couldn't have cared less. I didn't want to be in the Teamsters because I hated unions, and always had. Plus, I took to the dispatcher's job like a groom to his bride and was really good at it.

Since I now knew all the routes, it was especially easy for me to dispatch the men, freight, and later, salespersons. I was in that capacity for about three to four months until I decided that the Emery manager was nothing more than a snitch. He made notes and sat at his desk across from mine all day doing, saying, and suggesting absolutely nothing useful in running the trucking company to deliver and pick up airfreight. So I had a meeting with the owner and told him to get the man out of my way. He spoke to the Emery management, and the so-called manager was let go. I remember him explaining that he had been with Emery for over twenty years, and he couldn't believe that he was being let go. I told him that he was let go because he was of no use. He didn't contribute anything to the betterment of the company with exception of being a snitch on nothing but made up complaints. He left and that's when I could really make some headway. I was made the terminal manager and made all the decisions after that promotion.

Emery had three salesmen working in the areas I oversaw trying to increase the freight. However, I sold more accounts than they did, just by doing a good to great service. That included being in touch with their company's management and providing their needs with top quality. I had an opportunity to get a very large account in Dobbs Ferry, NY. The lead salesperson had been unable to get the account even though I had set up appointments for him. I called up the management of Emery and requested another salesperson since the three I had were somewhat worthless in my opinion. They sent me a woman who had the ability and desire to achieve, instead of complaining, and giving reasons why they couldn't do the job efficiently. I sent her into the Dobbs Ferry Company as her first sales undertaking, and she sold the services. She then continued to outsell all three of the salesmen combined. So I made another call and two were gone from my area and went to another. Hopefully Alaska! She and I quadrupled the airfreight coming out of that area in just five years.

Road rage on the Tappan Zee Bridge

This chapter is about road rage. First of all, I think that road rage got its origin in New York. Think about eight million people living and driving on an island that is twenty miles long and two miles wide. I had to go through it recently to get to LaGuardia airport, which was a nightmare of stopped traffic. I know that California has and had the greatest number of citizens. In fact, I lived in California between 1978 and 2010 and don't miss that traffic either.

It's around 1970 in NYC and traffic is a horror. Everyone is cutting off each other, passing on the right, beeping their horns, road problems, and toll booths, causing delays, and everybody in a hurry to get to wherever they were going.

At this time of life, my wife and I are living in an apartment in Sparkhill, NY. We have our baby son "Charlie" with us and we're there because it's the easiest way for me to drive to my trucking terminal, located in NY where I'm the terminal manager. The drive takes about an hour when the traffic is light.

The Teamsters union was giving me problems. Let me digress... I'm always having union problems. It's just that this was an extra hard time with the unions. So my attitude is not on the good side. I'm getting onto the Tappan Zee Bridge with a new Ford station wagon the business had leased for me for doing a good job. The car was a loaded station wagon because I had a family now, and a very nice car for a station wagon.

As I get onto the bridge, I always get directly to the left lane because it's where I'm likely to go the fastest and get through the toll booths the quickest. The Tappan Zee Bridge is usually extremely busy in the morning with cars waiting to get through the toll booths in all lanes a long way back.

I'm following traffic and thinking about business, my wife, my kid, who knows? When this guy in a small car moves from my right-side lane, straight in front of me. He doesn't have enough room to do so; thus, he forces me to go off the road to the left side nearly making me crash into the guardrail. I hit my brakes and nearly create an accident with the guy behind me.

Now, the real problem is I have a very hard time with people getting into my space, especially if it could cause damage or injury. So I hit the horn and this guy gives me the finger! Not a good choice on his behalf! I hate it when someone gives me the finger, unless, that is, they want to stop and discuss it on the side of the road! Then, I'm happy to discuss it. So I immediately start waving my thumb toward the right side, to tell this mutt, to pull over so we can discuss the finger issue and his terrible driving. But we especially need to see if he wants to back up his "f—— you" to me. He's not having any of it, because he's obviously a punk besides being a selfish mutt that doesn't care what happens to others as long as he's happy.

He gives me the finger again, thinking there's nothing I can do. He's probably been getting away with this all his life. Well, this was a very bad move because we would all soon be slowing to a stop as we approached the toll booths. So I stayed right behind him.

When we stopped, I jumped out and ran up to his car, telling him to get out. He already had locked the doors and with a big smile, gave me the finger again. Now I was absolutely livid! I yelled for him to get out and all he did was smile, flipping me off repeatedly. Now I could have just broken his window and dragged him out of it, since he'd locked the doors, but I immediately came up with a better idea. One that I wanted him to remember the rest of his life, and believe me, he still does.

First, I did a spinning roundhouse kick into his door, which put a huge dent in it and actually completely destroyed it. Remember we didn't have cell phones in those days, so he was screwed. No photos, no calls to the police, no help. Then I jumped up onto his hood and jumped up and down until the hood was bent around the engine destroying it. I was looking at him through the windshield while I was doing it and saw the look of complete fear and knowledge of his mistake on his face. I wasn't laughing or smiling. I'm sure my face had the look of hatred on it. That felt so good that I jumped up on top of his roof. Jumping up and down on it until it was making him bend over. I thought that I may as well make it a complete work of art, so I did the same to his trunk.

His car was completely ruined, but the taillights were still not damaged, which bothered me. Surprisingly, he was able to get the car started again, and slowly started moving forward, with the traffic, trying to get away from this maniac that was jumping around on and destroying his new car.

As he was inching forward, I kicked out his rear taillights and turned around to go to my car. I felt like King Kong, and now it was a "good morning." And it was also a real release from my anger and frustrations that I'd been going through with the Teamsters Union and my drivers. I don't think I could say the same for the mutt who gave me the finger.

On the way back to my car, which, as it sat there creating further traffic problems and stirring up honking, I noticed two huge black men standing next to the car doors of a new Cadillac. At first, I thought that they were pissed at me and I would have to defend myself. But as I came closer, I saw that they were holding their stomachs, because they were laughing so hard, they couldn't talk. Finally, when I got to my car, which was directly in front of theirs, one of them said, "I ain't never seen nothin' like that in all my born days. I don't know what he did, but I hope to hell I don't do it too. You is one crazy out yo mind guy! But I'm glad to have seen it, so's I can share it with ma friends, but I doubt that they will ever believe me, anyways." And believe me, I was really glad that they were not pissed at me.

Miraculously, even despite the lack of cell phones, I never heard a thing about this incident after I left the scene. This, of course, wasn't the only bit of road rage that I had in those days, but it was definitely one of the funniest to me. I have always hated when someone would give me the finger and had pulled more than one man out of his window, punching him in the face because of it. That's not pride you hear, it's just a fact. Truthfully, we are all wound up so tight with the life we are living at times. And if you had something to say then just back it up. If you can't or won't back it up, then put that finger in your mouth and shut your trap.

Here's an occurrence that brought out my anger! I had a guy come to my office in Rye, NY, one afternoon to sell me some supposedly stolen jewelry. I've now been around enough to know good and bad jewelry, or clothing. The jewelry he showed me was good, like a Rolex watch. I purchased the watch. But a little while after he left, I was looking at the watch and saw that he had switched the Rolex for a Bolex. Not a good thing. He wasn't gone long so I told my dispatcher to hold the fort and after jumping in my car drove to the nearest city, which was Port Chester, New York. I drove through town hoping that he went there to scam some other people in one of the stores or just on the street. And there he was! I was able to park a few spaces in front of him and walked back where he was trying to sell some men's jewelry to some guy on the sidewalk. As I was walking up to him, I said to the guy, "Don't buy any of his shit because he's a liar and a thief who swaps the jewelry when you go for your wallet." No longer interested in buying his goods, the would-be customer/sucker immediately turned and walked swiftly away.

The guy who switched the watch on me started to say something when I punched him in the face, and he fell to the ground. I grabbed his arm and helped him up walking him over to his parked car. He didn't even think of retaliating, just decided to shut up and listen and hope he didn't get another punch. I told him to give me my money back and was going to have him give me the Rolex also. But someone had called the police and a police car pulled up alongside of us. The cop got out and walked over asking what was going on. He said he'd received a call that there was a fight on the street, and he was betting it was us. I immediately said that we were friends that haven't seen one another for years and when we met, we must have looked like we were fighting, but we were just messing around. He looks at the other guy and sees that the side of his face is red and starting to swell. He asks him why his face appears to be hurt. The guy looks at me and says to the cop that we were just fooling around, and it was a mistake that he got hurt. Then he wisely says whoever saw us and called the police, will also confirm that right after I got hurt by mistake, my buddy here helped me up off the sidewalk. The policeman said, "You two had better stop fooling around or I will bring you in for disturbing the peace at a minimum." We agreed to comply and he left. By that time I had my money back, he got a punch to the face, and I just left him without demanding he give me the Rolex feeling he might say no, and then I would wind up being arrested FOR SURE.

Anthony's Road Rage

Well, that was one of my road rage incidents but let me tell you of one that Anthony "Hickey" had on the West Side Highway one day.

It was early one morning, and Anthony was on his way into the city driving south on the West Side Highway. Anthony was dealing with a lot of problems due to a pending indictment and continuous news coverages concerning his involvement in the Genovese crime circle, and other legal issues. He was in the slow lane and not concentrating on what was going on around him. Suddenly, there was a guy in a car directly behind him beeping his horn and suggesting that he pulls over to the side of the road.

Anthony had no idea what made this guy so mad. So he just tries to continue and ignore this guy, because he certainly doesn't need to have another charge against him for beating this mutt up. Especially, since he has no idea what got him so upset in the first place.

Well, the guy doesn't stop suggesting that Anthony should pull over with hand actions and beeping the horn. That's really an unimaginably bad decision for this guy, and I don't care who he is. Anthony has had enough of his challenges, and he pulls over to the side of the highway where there is a slight pull out, between the West Side Highway and the Hudson River. The guy pulls directly up behind him. Anthony gets out at the same time this guy gets out and briskly walks toward him.

As he gets to within reach of the guy, he reaches out and grabs this guy by the front lapels. He starts dragging this guy, who he has pulled off his feet, toward the Hudson River, so he can throw him into it. All the while this guy is really being dragged by his camera strap that he had put around his neck. He's trying to yell and tell

66

Anthony that he wasn't challenging him; he just wanted to have him stop so he could take Anthony's picture. He was a news magazine journalist who recognized Anthony and wanted to interview him and take his photo for the cover of Time magazine.

Anthony finally listens as he's dragging this journalist toward the river to toss him in. He is beyond angry and hasn't been listening. So when he finally understands what this guy is trying to do, he stops, helps the guy up, and straightens this guy's clothing before standing back so his photo can be taken with a big smile on his face. "This is a true story" and it can be proved by looking up the Time magazine cover page where Anthony is standing in front of the Hudson River, with the West Side highway behind him. This photo can only have been taken from the side of the West Side Highway near the river. There are no areas along the highway for this to have been taken, unless the cars had been pulled over to do so.

The front-page cover photo is of Anthony wearing his favorite custom blue leather jacket that matches his 1972 Mercedes 450SL convertible.

Here's the thing that you should understand and remember. Even though a man has been put in prison for assault. It doesn't mean that he will never do that again. A person who has the instinct to use physical force is always inclined to do it. You think about it and the results to you that may incur for beating a man, but when you believe he needs a beating, he gets one.

Sometimes when the TV shows a man kicking another who is down on the ground the viewer thinks, "I can't believe he is kicking him, when he seems defenseless." But the viewer probably never had to fight for their lives. The reason you kick a guy when he is down is because that's why you put him on the ground is so that you can kick him! Getting in a fight with someone in NYC means that you are determined that the other guy remembers to never mess with you again. We also wanted to end it quickly, avoiding undue punches to ourselves. People often saw my size and really wanted the challenge of trying to take me down. I didn't go around starting fights, but I'd be sure to stick that message in the mind of the guys who were dumb enough to go there with me. Just stay out of my way or be friendly.

Card Games, Pool Games, Life Gains

I was included in some card games that were very private and occasionally dangerous because of the men invited. We actually didn't use the term "Wise Guys" as used by other writers, however, since the term is so widely understood, I will use it for this episode in my life.

These card games were held in the same places where we were served drinks and sandwiches and the door was locked and sometimes "covered" by one of us who was sitting out. We had better know who you are when you approach the entry door, or you weren't getting in no matter what. Keep in mind that gambling in New York was illegal, which made it all the more fun. Should the police have come and tried to enter they would have had to break the door down and all the money would have been off the table before they got in.

They never tried mainly because they knew who we were. So many people were paid off to let us do what we wanted to do, anyway. Back then the police, the captains, anyone in control, like the mayor, or even judges were all taking money so that illegal things could be done with no repercussions.

There was a movie made in 1972 called Serpico. If you've seen that movie you know how it was. A straight cop, Serpico, is hated by other cops because he wouldn't be part of their taking bribe money so that crimes like dealing drugs or running numbers and a myriad of other crimes could be done with no problems. It was rampant! In fact, one of the reasons why I could accept what I was doing, was because I didn't see myself as crooked as the cops who thought that they were moral. To me, here were people who are being paid off so that other people could escape the law, which made them even more criminal than me, in my opinion then.

Interestingly enough I remember that the gambling locale was upstairs next to a stairwell where there were "accidents" involving persons who somehow fell down the stairs and would later claim that they were pushed or thrown. So now the question is how someone could be part of the game and then be thrown down the stairs? Because someone who was part of "us" brought them in, thinking that they would fit, being quiet and playing the game without complaint if they lost. But it turned out that they were bad losers and definitely did not fit in. So there were those who needed to know if they could fly.

One-time Anthony's brother "Moon" threw a man down some stairs. His brother was known as "Moon" and he wasn't a big man, but he could more than handle himself, very well. I remember one time when he threw a guy down a flight of stairs at a high-end restaurant we always went to, and sometimes played cards in the rear private room. But he was thrown out of the restaurant because he was a mafia leader in New Jersey. He was a real nut case that liked to end problems by having someone killed. He was told that if he was seen in NYC or the five boroughs, that would be his last day on earth. He stayed in New Jersey and Moon lived to be an old man. Not necessarily because that guy was fearful of Moon, but because he was associated with the Genovese Mafia. Which was a very respected crime family, and "Moon" was "Hickey's" brother.

There was a very private, illegal, and secured casino located in Whitestone, NY, that operated only on the weekends, to my knowledge. It was located in an abandoned building near the Whitestone Bridge and I believe was previously some type of school. Apparently, the cops, the mayor, and possibly the judges were paid off to allow the casino to operate. The parking lot was large and dark since the only lights were the muted glow coming from the highway. There was a pair of wired-glass steel doors that were locked with a couple of armed men standing inside the doors to let you in, only if you were *known,* of course. Only "associated" (or wise guys) and their wives or women friends, or an occasional trusted friend were allowed to gamble there. Or if you were with someone like "Hickey" who carried enough weight that the doors opened as soon as he approached them, allowing whoever was with him to have immediate entry also.

Everyone was asked to hang their weapons on the sidewall until they left. Even though the place was filled with criminals, no one ever had their weapon taken by mistake or otherwise. The ramifications of stealing from one another could have been lethal. First, you wanted your own piece. Second, you wouldn't know if you were stealing someone like Anthony's that would bring down a whole lot of shit on your head. Actually, it was rare for Anthony or anyone like him that had a criminal record like his to carry. Once you were found guilty and incarcerated you could be detained and patted down at any time. If you were found with a weapon you would be back in the clink, pronto. So such men kept others with them should protection be needed. If they thought that they needed to carry, bet your life on it.

I remember when an associate had just gotten out of prison on parole for a short time and the FBI forced their way into his apartment and searched the entire place. They didn't need a warrant, because of his parole. They found a large pocketknife in bedroom drawer. They immediately threw the cuffs on him and he finished out his term, because of a pocketknife in his drawer at his home. What we knew, as did they, is that he used a knife, when hired, to kill people.

Getting back to the casino, after entry we walked down a dark hallway with doors that appeared to be classrooms on either side. Then, we reached a set of steel doors that opened up into a large room that looked like a Las Vegas casino. There were huge crystal chandeliers, expensive wallpapered walls, high-end decorated carpeting, and a catwalk that ran around the top of the room's perimeter. The catwalk originally was presumably used for indoor running built in earlier years. But now men with weapons stood by as a kind of, let's say, insurance or security. The room was filled with card tables, roulette, blackjack and craps tables, you name it. Although it was busy, it wasn't especially crowded. There were men and a few women who were throwing money around like they were all so rich that their loss or their winnings made no difference. They were there merely for the excitement of the moment or in some cases due to their gambling addictions. In general, and typically, it really didn't matter because most of them were playing with other people's money, often acquired illegally. I've said it before and repeat it again. Illegal money had to be hidden, it couldn't be put in the bank for any authorities to discover and want to know where it came from.

The first night that I was there Anthony pointed out a woman who was associated in some way and was also respected. One story about her is that she supposedly peed in her pants one evening while sitting at a blackjack table because she didn't want to leave her spot and break her winning streak. Anthony said she won around 250K that night and everyone laughed at her tenacity to stay in her seat, while putting up with her personal embarrassment. She had stated that she thought she could hold it but was surprised when the fight was lost. So when she was finished gambling, she wrapped her coat around her and walked out of the building with most people not knowing anything.

Remember when imagining this scene that wise guys were always dressed to the hilt with the latest custom-tailored suits, shirts, ties, shoes, and jewelry. The women typically wore evening dresses, except for the cocktail waitresses, who wore nearly nothing. Anthony told me that he had never brought anyone else there with him. That did not mean that other associates of his had not been there, but that they had been there on their own, or someone else had brought them. I felt very special that he trusted me to go there with him. And I also knew he was full of shit.

As usual, he was pretty quiet as to who knew about or owned this place, and of course I didn't ask since it was none of my business. I went there with him only that one time, because quite frankly I didn't know if I could get entry without him. I probably could have, but the place seemed to be a little too much for me. The truth is, I always enjoyed a more private card game than putting my money up against different odds like the house. This place was like Las Vegas where the expenses of "the house" were covered by the gambler's losses. Later in life, when I was in Las Vegas, I always realized that the beautiful buildings and furnishings were not paid for with the winnings of the clientele, hence the odds! I was also a small fish in a big pond when it came to the amount of money that everyone was throwing around, especially Anthony.

We left that evening around midnight and went into Manhattan to meet with Mersh, Philly "Brush," Jackie "the Nose" and Anthony's brother "Moon." We met in a small bar that had a rear room for us to meet and discuss the trucking business, unions, as well as other business issues. When we were finished with our business, Anthony suggested that we go have a drink at the bar. Although the bar and the restaurant were already closed, it was not unusual for us to determine if a place was open or closed—it was on our time, not theirs. They knew who we were, and they wanted the business that we brought in, along with the protection that they were given once their place became known as one of the hangouts.

The bartender and a rather large Irish-looking man were playing pool when we came out of the back room. The bartender saw us and immediately left the pool game to get us whatever we wanted. While we were ordering, the bartender asked me if I wanted to continue his game for him, since he's busy getting drinks for everyone. Anthony agreed that I should, although he challenged me by suggesting that "*I may not know how to handle a stick.*" He asked if I had ever touched one. I joked, "Which way do you hold the stick, fat end or thin?" And everyone laughed, with exception of that six-foot-eight, three-hundred-plus-pound, red-haired Irishman. I'm guessing those statistics because he was taller and heavier than my six-foot-five, 250-pound frame.

I went to the table and asked whose turn it was. The Irishman, Mickey says, "Who the f— said you could play pool with me, ya little shit?" I stood back to assess the situation believing that this was another set up by Anthony in front of all his pals/business partners. They all gave out a short laugh, and although I never took my eyes off the Irishman, I knew they were all looking at me, and that they all were in on it. Just as he was about to say something I said, "Well, to be honest, the bartender over there suggested that I take his place. But now I see that you're too scared to play against me, and that you're a f...ing big mouth asshole. So maybe I'll leave you to play with yourself, which I'm sure you've had plenty of experience with."

He then took a step forward and took a purposeful swing at me with his pool stick. One thing I'd learned in life (and in my karate classes) is that you don't swing at someone with a club, bat, or pool stick. That's because if you miss while you are backing out of range, it puts you in a precarious position while your arms and body are affected by the inertia of the swing. In this case I reacted, and he did miss. At that very moment I used the thick end of my pool stick and drove it directly into his solar plexus (area of the abdomen just below the ribcage which is full of nerve fibers), doubling him over with a loud grunt, unable to breathe. Then I used an upward movement of the pool cue (to the forehead) which drove his head up, painfully. Lastly, I drove the pool cue into his forehead with a quick, hard snap, knocking him backward onto his ass, on the floor. He slowly got to his knees and was holding his stomach and his forehead, probably wondering if it was me who had been set up, or him. I backed up, waiting for some kind of reaction from him as he stood up, but none came. After about half a minute, I asked him if this pool game was over and he pretty much, convincingly, said that he didn't wish to continue. I backed away, never taking my eyes off him and reached for my drink.

As I was bringing it off the bar and raising it toward my mouth, Anthony who was directly next to me raised his and said, "Here, here, everybody—let's give a well-done toast to Charlie." They all put their drinks in their right hand, because a left-handed toast is considered an insult to the one that is being honored and drank to me.

Mickey was slowly coming around to normal when I asked him if he would like to have a drink with us. To my surprise he said, "Certainly." He ordered a drink on me, and stood there with a look of confusion, trying to figure out how in the world the tables had turned. Since he was so much bigger and apparently had lots of experience with bar fights. He undoubtedly had been paid to bust my ass in front of everyone, or better yet to make me back down and walk out. A test like that is often done to see what a man is made of. It was my turn! He outweighed me at that time by about forty to fifty pounds, but he didn't know, and neither did any of the rest of them, that I had been training in karate four to five nights a week between leaving the trucking terminal and either going home or into the city to meet on other "business." I loved training for karate and was fast and somewhat proficient at that time.

We had no further issues and I never saw him again. However, as he was leaving Anthony stopped him and digging into his suit pocket pulled out three $100 bills and handed it to him saying, "This is for your troubles." I knew it was a payoff for what he had owed him, trying to kick my ass. Anthony later admitted it to me, when we were on the lam up in Canada after his escape, along with a few other even more surprising details. He said that he and everybody there needed to see what I would do and if I could handle myself.

My "Rep"

Well, first of all, I need to admit that I had a really hard time sharing this with anyone, especially everyone who reads this. Things like this were not discussed with your friends or your relatives or especially your wife (wives) and kids. All who really knew me back then knew that I had a bad temper. They knew that I was also struggling for identification of who I was. They knew that I could definitely defend myself. They also knew that I would protect them with my life. They knew that I was definitely involved with the Mafia, besides running trucking companies and dealing with the Teamsters union. They especially knew because I was now the son-in-law of the Genovese under boss. But they also knew that I had a great sense of humor and was liked for it. I really had few friends; I had family, and those who I was associated with in business. The bottom line to this thought, is that few alive today know this story, and it's hard to tell because I'm not the person who I used to be, and don't want to be thought of as the person in this chapter. However, I still feel the same way about pimps and drug dealers. We never had anything to do with drugs. If there were any drug dealings, I would not be part of the organization, even in running the trucking companies.

Well, here it is! I was in downtown NYC with Anthony one evening with a few business associates eating dinner and discussing the trucking business and union problems as usual. When it was over and we were drinking at the bar, one of the men there said he was going to go to a card game with some other friends at an apartment downtown. Anthony questioned me, "Why don't you go with him?" because he knew how much I liked to play cards. I knew this guy but was not on close friendly terms with him, but my first thought was "Okay." My second thought was, "I wonder if I've pissed someone off and this is just to get my butt downtown and out of sight temporarily or for good." You just never knew how long you were useful or even really liked. Although everyone knew that I liked to play cards, I accepted, and we drove to another location downtown together in my car. This guy lived in the same neighborhood as where the card game was being held, and he didn't have his car up at the restaurant since someone had brought him to the restaurant where we had just been.

We played cards for a few hours and I still had to drive from downtown to my home in Montvale, New Jersey, which was easily an hour ride without any traffic or delays at that time. It was somewhere around one in the morning and I decided to take off along with Tommy, the guy that I'd gone to play cards with. We went downstairs and while I was heading for my car and he was heading to his home, which was only a block away, all hell broke out! That's when I heard this screaming and yelling coming from an alley between the building we were in and the next building. When I walked over, I saw this guy punching this tiny blond girl that couldn't have been more than sixteen years old. Tommy said to me, "That guy is a local pimp and a drug dealing creep." Tommy intended to continue on his way and mind his own business, when I said to him "I f…ing hate pimps and drug dealers," and men who hit women.

So I continued walking into the alley to stop this scumbag from punching this kid and teach him some manners. If I ever learned one thing from my parents, it was that a man NEVER hits women, under any circumstances. Now I know that the people I was associated with were known to hit their wives and children at times. However, I never saw it happen, and I'm glad because I probably would have intervened with them also. Which may not have turned out so well with me.

Anyway, I grabbed this Mutt by the back of his jacket, surprising him as I turned him around in one swift move. When he was facing me, I hit him in the nose with what is called in Japanese "Uracken showmen uchi" or inverted strike to the face. Which breaks the nose and fills the eyes full of blood at the same time impairing his vision and setting him up for the next strike that's already on its way, which

I was always was taught to deliver. Always do a follow up with a minimum of a second punch, strike, or kick. That was followed by a short fist strike to the solar plexus (called Seiken chudan tsuki.) Then, I picked him up while knocking the wind out of him and bending him over gasping for air. I really didn't like this pimp, girl, kid beater. Then I brought my knee up into his face "Hiza geri" and broke his nose further. With this it sprang him up with force and I did what is called "Higi." This action is an elbow strike coming up to the jaw that can dislocate or break the jaw. (I always wanted to try that move on someone ever since learning how to do it in karate classes.) He went on the ground trying to breathe through a broken nose and jaw. The deflated diaphragm made it extra hard. I started to have compassion for him... NOT. I'd have continued only the object never was to kill him, just to teach karate to him through a learning experience, because he needed to learn how not to be a woman-beating-pimp-scumbag.

At this time, he was no problem, so I turned my attention to the girl who was leaning over in pain but looking up at me with huge open eyes of fear, probably wondering if she was next. I helped her up and told her she had nothing to fear and asked her why he was beating her up. She said that she didn't bring in enough money doing tricks for him today. I said so he's your pimp. She said yes, with a very embarrassed look on her face. I asked her where she was from. She told me she had run away from her home in "somewhere" Idaho and came here on buses to get as far away as she could. I asked her how long she had been doing tricks for this scumbag. She said only about two months.

At this time, I saw the pimp reaching into his pocket for, I assumed, his pistol. I knew he would be carrying but wanted him to do something stupid, so that I could continue the teaching, and unloose my anger. So I kicked his arm right at the elbow and nearly broke his arm at the elbow. After that scream, I told him if he screams or talks again, I will see to it that he is out cold. I bent down and took a .38-caliber snub nose pistol out of his jacket pocket and stuck it in my coat pocket. I also pushed him down and reached into his pocket and found $200 and put it in my pocket.

I then asked the girl if she wanted to get away from this guy. She said, "Yes." I realized what she was thinking and told her that I wasn't a pimp; in fact, I hated pimps, and drug dealers which was part of the reason why I beat up this woman-beating, drug-dealing scumbag. I asked her if she really wanted to stay in this city where she would always be a tool for someone to use because of her age, beauty, and innocence.

She told me a story common with kids running away from home. She didn't have any money or anywhere to stay when he approached her within minutes of her getting off the bus and bought her some dinner. Dinner became a place to stay she thought temporarily, until it became a type of prison. She said she'd been thinking and praying that she would like to have gone home right after she was forced to do tricks for this guy. But never had the nerve or the money to do so. She said at first, he was very nice to her and appeared like he wanted to help her by giving her a place to stay, as he told her, with no strings attached, until she found some work. Then she made the mistake of sleeping with him, when she couldn't find work and he had been so nice to her. It turned out one night after having sex with him and getting high on marijuana and cocaine, she was forced to sleep with another man right in the same bed. After that he forced her to work for him by keeping her broke and smacking her around, making her have sex with other men, unless he told her, she wanted to have her pretty face rearranged.

That's when I reached into my pocket and pulled out the two hundred dollars I had taken from this pimp and handed it to her. I said I really hope that you'll take this and go home. Get the hell out of this hellhole and go back to your parents. I asked if she ran away because they were harmful or abusive to her physically in any way. She said no, while turning her head to look down in embarrassment and again, realizing what a mistake she had made of her life. She told me that she had gotten into some trouble for cutting some classes in school with her boyfriend and thought that her parents were being too restrictive with her punishment. So she left. I asked her if they were as restrictive and cruel as this asshole lying on the pavement.

She didn't have to answer that; we both knew the answer. It was more of a prompt than a question.

I then asked if she needed to get any belongings like clothing or anything from where she was staying. She said she had some clothing in his apartment because that's where she has been staying since she came into town. But she was afraid to go there. I asked her where the apartment was. She told me it was in the building next to the alley we were in. I said come with me and show me where it is, meaning with me and this scumbag. However, I didn't realize that Tommy was actually still there with me in the alley. He was so quiet just standing behind me watching my back at the entrance of the alley, I wasn't even aware that he was there. I immediately liked this guy and handed him the confiscated .38 on my way toward the building entrance.

I grabbed this guy's unbroken arm under his armpit and hoisted him up standing (as best he could) and said, "Take me to your apartment, now." He was in no shape to argue and probably wanted to get into his apartment, anyway, thinking that he could lie down and call a friend to get him to a hospital. He possibly even wanted to call the police when I left. He lived on the third floor and the building had no elevator, so he really was hating life on the way up. I had some real compassion for him then, again… "NOT!" Screw him, he was lucky to be able to go to his apartment.

He gave me his key and we went into his apartment which was actually pretty nice, for a low life punk like him. I found out from the kid that he had a few other girls in his harem, downtown. This increased my love for the guy immensely. I saw a bunch of white powder in a bowl on the living room coffee table and walked over and picked it up. I asked him what it was, and he mumbled through his broken jaw that it was Coke. So I then walked over to the kitchen sink and washed it down the sink. I asked him where his other drugs were. He said that was all he had, so I smacked him in his face with the back of my hand and asked him again. I remember hoping that he refused to tell me again. This scumbag was not only a woman beater and a pimp, but also a drug dealer who has caused unbelievable and unforgiveable pain to not only his girls, but the kids he'd turned into drug addicts. He told me he had his stash in his bedroom closet under some floorboards.

Well, the kid (Lisa was her name) packed her belongings in a paper bag, and was ready to go when I stopped her and asked, "Don't you have a suitcase or something?" She nervously said no, and I told her to go and get his and pack her things in it, so she didn't have to look like a vagabond traveling with a paper bag. I asked if she'd had a suitcase when she arrived. And she told me she did but had to sell to help make her quota with him. All she wanted to do was get out of the city because she thought that he would still find her. I insisted that she get his suitcase and put her thing in it to travel with. While she was exchanging her clothing into the suitcase, I asked her if he knew where she was from. She said only that she was from Idaho and nothing else because he really didn't care to know more about her, other than how to control her with fear.

Then it hit me that this scumbag must have a stash of cash somewhere. While I was with her in the bedroom getting her clothes, and Tommy in the kitchen watching this mutt, I asked Lisa if she knew where his money was. She said in a small wall safe behind boxes on the shelf in the closet. Well, now I'm in this scumbag's kitchen and he's sitting in a kitchen chair where I put his ugly ass, being watched by Tommy.

I asked him where he kept his money hidden. His eyes opened wide, and said he didn't have a place where he stashed money. I snickered and said, "Apparently you really haven't figured out who you're dealing with. Do you think that I'm some mooch that doesn't know better than that? Everybody in this town, and every town in America, that is making dough through illegal means must hide their money. So where is it? And before you say you don't have a stash here again; think about how much pain you can endure?"

This idiot says he really doesn't have a stash. He says that he spent all his money on the stash of drugs in his closet, and that he had told me where that was. Well, not only do I know different, but I'm glad that he said he didn't, so I could cause more pain to this scumbag drug-dealing pimp. I was on a trip to get all my hate for people like him, out on him, right then. It wasn't only a punk like him, but the scum that were on drugs spitting on the hero soldiers coming home from putting their lives on the line, defending our country in Viet Nam. Guys like him, holding rallies and going to concerts where scum like him were selling while on drugs themselves. I hated drugs and still do!

I did a side sweep of his chair that he was sitting on with my foot and knocked him out of the chair and onto the floor, landing on his now bad arm that I think may have been broken because of the fall. He lets out a scream of pain through his broken jaw and I react with a stomp on his leg that is still resting over the turned over chair. Oop's, his leg was now definitely broken! I went into his kitchen cabinets and found an unopened bottle of Scotch. Tommy and I had a couple of shots and then he woke up. When he comes to, I asked him, where is the stash? He refused to answer because he didn't want to tell me where, not knowing that I already knew, and probably thinking that I'll off him after I know. He's totally afraid what could happen next with this maniac (me). He's just about out of it in pain.

I got down on one knee and put my thumb onto a place between his nose and his eyeball, explaining that I know exactly how to pull out his eyeball with little effort. And he'll be looking down at the floor with the one eye that's hanging out, until the other one is taken out too. If he didn't tell me where it was, that's probably what would have happened. But I don't have to take out his eye…too bad. I should have done it just because of what he has been doing to kids. He tells me it's in a wall safe that he installed, in his closet, verifying what Lisa had told me in the bedroom.

I went to it and after finding it, went back into the kitchen, to ask him what the code is. He hesitated, but he wisely mumbled it out when I started walking toward him with a smile on my face. I think it finally got to him that not only was I not to fool with, but it was VERY personal.

I opened the safe and there was 30K there all wrapped up neatly in hundred-dollar bills, and ready for me. I also obtained the stash of drugs that he had hidden in the floor at the same time. The first thing I did when returning to the kitchen was to pour all the drugs down the sink with running water. He was now moaning not in pain but pure fear, since (and I knew) that his stash was probably not paid for. Now he would deal with some other scum dealing trash that might kill him, if he didn't convince them that he would come up with the cash, and he wouldn't be seeming very convincing to anyone at this point.

Lisa was still in the room watching all this when I realized that she needed to get on her way. I peeled off another three hundred dollars from his cash and gave it to her. I told her she should go to Newark New Jersey and get on a plane and go home. I told her to get out of here and go home and continue the life that she ran away from. I said that she didn't have to worry about this asshole coming to find her, because I would take care of anything like that. I told her she didn't have to share everything with her parents if she thought it would really hurt them. But to definitely go to some kind of a counselor and share her experiences so she could get some help in dealing with the life she had been forced to live here. I assured her that counselor would not discuss it with any one if she asked them not to.

I suggested that she go to the bus stop or subway and leave this city as soon as she could so that no one else could get to her. Putting definite fear and excitement into her, she left, after giving me a huge hug and kissing my cheek, thanking me and Tommy. I assumed that she was getting on a bus or the subway that goes into New Jersey where she could get to the airport to take her home. I couldn't help her since I didn't and still don't take busses or subways, so I knew nothing about them, or where to catch them. She knew how and she left, never to return to my knowledge. I must believe and hope that she returned home and was welcomed with open arms and lot of forgiveness and love. In meeting her for that short time, I believed she deserved a better life.

So now comes the part that I really loved. I grabbed the pimp with his broken leg and arm and sat him onto another chair at the kitchen table. I sat next to him and explained a few things to him in a very quiet and calm voice. I had learned that angle from Anthony. I said, with a smile, "My name is Charlie and here's the deal… I hate drug dealers and pimps with a complete passion as I imagine you've guessed by now. I'm taking your money, so thanks for the 30K, but

I'm not keeping a dime." He turned his head a little like he didn't understand if he heard correctly. "What I'm going to do," I continued, "is give it to some of my associates. If anything happens to me, this guy next to me, Lisa or any of your other girls that were under your control, these associates of mine will gladly come and find you. And this is the only the beginning of what you'll go through should I or he have some kind of accident, before you meet all your friends in Hell."

I explained that I'm a crazy driver and I might get into an accident just because of my driving. But guess what? If that happens, they are going think that you were involved, and they'd come for you for retribution. "You do know what retribution means don't you? It's exactly what you're thinking right now. It is revenge. I am part of their business let's say, and worth money to them, so they would be really upset if anything would happen to me or to him." I pointed to Tommy with my thumb over my shoulder. "And you will be the guy they look for. In fact, one of my associates "I've heard" likes to cut things up with a knife. He thinks he's an artist with a knife! By the way, if you or any of your friends think that you can get to us, think again because I'm associated with the Genovese Mafia. And my father-in-law is well known as their underboss at this time. You've seen him in the news. His name is Anthony Hickey DiLorenzo. So here's the deal! I suggest that you tell everyone that you fell down those steps outside which caused all these health problems. You'll have to tell something because you'll need help just getting to the hospital. Then there will be months of healing. And you'll have to explain how you're going to repay those scumbags that let you have those drugs, which are now on their way to the sewer. I highly suggest that while you're healing you get your scumbag ass out of this town, this state, and the neighboring states. Not just because you won't be able to pay them back soon enough, but because if I happen to see you again, let's say at a dinner in New Jersey, I'll probably think that you planned it, to get back at me. So I'll have to react in self-defense with a real passion of getting to know you again."

Then we left. I gave $4,700 to Tommy for watching my back and then drove home that night. Tommy was a real stand-up guy who knew the score. He knew he had nothing to worry about because we all also had his back. If anyone even looked sideways at him because of this, we would be down on them like a sledgehammer on glass.

On my drive home, there was no remorse, no sorrow, no fear, just feeling really good that I was able to be there and help Lisa return to her home. Coming out of that building when this scumbag was hitting that little girl, was unlucky for him. The next day after I was done at my trucking company, I went into town and met with Anthony. He wasn't aware of anything that had occurred the night before and I needed to tell him before he heard it from anyone else. He was funny that way!

I gave him 15K of the 25K left after giving Tommy his 4.5K, and Lisa $500. I explained how I got it and why I was giving it to him. As always, he laughed and said, "You really are a f...ing nutcase, aren't you?"

I said, "No, I just hate pimps, drug dealers, and men hitting women."

We were then having drinks when Philly Brush walks in. I bought him and Anthony a drink and gave Philly 5K. He looks at me and asks what this is for? I start to explain and Moersch walks in. I wasn't sure who the last guy would be. When he walked in, I bought him a drink and handed him the last 5K. I always liked Moersch more than any of the guys I was involved with other than Anthony, because he was a true "standup guy."

I then explained everything to them all, and they said the exact same thing that Anthony has said, you really are f...ing nuts. I said no I'm not nuts, I just hate pimps and drug dealers, especially when they're hitting some young girl. They cracked up when I said I also needed and enjoyed practicing my karate on him. I asked if they would follow up on what I told this Mutt should there be any retribution on me or Tommy. Thinking more of the drug dealers who now lost their drugs, than this punk I took them from. They agreed and said that I didn't even have to give them the money, and they would have my back anyway. But I told them that I really didn't want any money that came from drugs or pimping, and we shook hands on everything.

They teased me the rest of the night, actually for years later about that incident. They would say…hey, have you seen any pimps lately, I could use some cash. Or I heard this one arm, one legged, one eyed, broken jawed, guy with a smashed nose was in here looking for you. I'd say, yea I saw a pimp the other day, did you see him with a suitcase running to get on a train or bus to get out of town. We'd have our laughs, and I never again saw or heard anything about this low life.

It was about a week later when Tommy met up with Anthony and told him his side of the incident. He told it just like I had told it. That's when Anthony realized that I had the qualifications to be counted on in other ways. Not just the unusual ability to run trucking outfits with profits, and solve union problems, but also other areas of business.

The bottom line to this is that neither I nor Tommy ever saw or heard anything about that scumbag again. He was smarter than I had originally thought, and probably got out of town before the next payment was due on the drugs, I'd flushed down the drain. Consequently, it gave my associates a different view and respect of who I could be to their network of businesses. Which at the time I thought was great! Because it gave me a reputation of physical abilities that had been unknown, with exception of the picketing at Breen in the beginning. Also, they realized my attitude that when needed I would "definitely do" what was needed.

Besides helping that kid Lisa with her pimp, I helped other random ladies a few times in bars or clubs when their husband or boyfriend would hit them. I would interfere and beat the scum unmercifully. I remember such an occurrence one time in a bar on the east side when I was having a conversation with an associate. This man smacked his wife across the face with the back of his hand and knocks her off her stool onto the floor. He's yelling at her and grabs her arm in an attempt to pick her up and give her another slap. I came at him while standing at that bar and broke his hold with a strike to the joint at the elbow. This hurt like hell, possibly nearly breaking his arm at the elbow. He let out a girlish scream and I grabbed his shirt with my right hand and backhanding him across his face as hard as I can with my left. He tried to protect himself with his other hand and I snapped that down and gave him another slap in the face with my palm this time. I continued to slap this woman-beater forcing him backward until he was up against the jukebox. That's when he went down onto his knees to trying to get away from me. While I still continued to smack this mutt with an open hand back and forth his wife gets up off the floor and is screaming for me to stop. When I did stop, she went over to him, helped him up and they both left, nearly running out the door.

As I went back to my seat to continue my conversation, the whole room is clapping and cheering, like they're at a ball game. The only problem was that my hand hurt so much and was so swollen that I couldn't even pick up my drink. The bartender saw it and brought me a towel with ice in it to put on my hand. The guy I was with had a smile on his face so big I almost didn't recognize him. Then he said to me, "You do know that you're a f——n' idiot, don't you?" I continued to look at him and said, "Yea, but I feel better now, than if I'd done nothing to that mutt." We had a drink and continued sharing our thoughts until we were finished, and I left. The other problem was that although all my associates knew how I felt about men hitting women, there were those who also hit their women. But thank God, they never did it in front of me, which is another reason why I know now that God has saved me, so many times.

After that meeting with Anthony, I did collections for him and for other associates that could use my services. Most of them had been incarcerated and didn't need or want to risk getting caught beating someone up for lack of payment. It was to my advantage because I used to get a percentage of the amount of money that I received from the borrowers. Then I would often put it back in the street doing the same thing as a loan shark myself. Only not in large amounts like the rest of them. Doing collections gave me acceptance by his associates. But running and increasing business in the trucking industry got me more respect than anything because of the profits that were associated with my businesses. And I was "really good" at managing trucking companies.

I got a request from Anthony one day asking me to locate a man who he had loaned a considerable amount of money to and had not received the agreed monthly vig for a few months. A vig is the interest on money loaned out by loan sharks. If the original loan amount was "paid 1887 in full" at any time and then the vig was canceled. I did the usual. I went to the bars, clubs, and restaurants asking if this guy had been there and to let me know if he showed up, also requesting that the word be passed around that Anthony and I were looking for him.

I was notified by an associate that the bartender located in Kennedy Airport called him and told him that the guy I was looking for, was in his bar waiting to board a flight out of the country. My office was in Kennedy Airport at the time and I went directly to the bar where I was told he was sitting. When this guy saw me, he turned green and forced a fake smile while getting up to supposedly welcome me with a handshake. I already knew that he was intending to escape and when I grabbed his hand for the handshake, I grabbed only two fingers and immediately broke them. He let out a painful yelp, while at the same time I warned him to keep quiet and sit down if he wanted to keep the remaining fingers and possibly more bones unbroken. He knew that the cops would not be called, by the bartender and immediately sat down. We had a short one-sided conversation when I was informed that the remaining money, he had borrowed was in his valise sitting next to him. He then attempted to explain why the loan had not been returned to Anthony along with the required back monthly vig that he also owed. I told him that he had better contact Anthony not me because Anthony was the only one who could give him absolution for his actions. I then took his airplane ticket and passport and told him to see Anthony to get them back. I returned the money that he had to Anthony and never had any further dealing with him either.

There were a few other similar deals with getting loaned money back that were similar in results although more painful results in some. Believe it or not, although I did do collections, I never really wanted to hurt anyone. After locating the guys who were in trouble for not paying their vig, or the amount loaned. I would try to reason with them to see (or should I say insist) they make amends. However, when one of them would attempt to come at me with violence. They got a beating that sometimes resulted in broken bones. That was their decision, not mine.

That's how I got my reputation with the underworld.

Start to Watch His Back

That was actually a lot more than just a test of courage and ability. It was what enlightened Anthony to have me "watch his back" in circumstances where he needed someone, he knew he could trust and who could be resourceful under immediate and pressing circumstances. It was also a test to see just how far I would go. Also, to see if I had the street smarts to realize that I was set up. You can't just trust someone because he's with someone else who is known. I became an integral part of the organizations trucking operations and needed to be tested. They all of course knew about my dealing with the drug dealing, pimp downtown, because Anthony, Philly, Mersh, and Moon were all given the cash from that situation. That incident was how I really got my reputation of anger and action.

Several weeks later, Anthony called me at my trucking terminal office in Rye, NY, and asks me to meet him at the local diner in about an hour. When I showed up, he asked me to accompany him in his car, a beautiful new Mercedes convertible. He always had beautiful new cars. In fact, we all did. It was part of the perks of living that life. The cars could all be traced back to legitimate businesses like the trucking companies I was running and involved with. We also drew salaries to cover our obvious expenses like our houses, clothing, and expenses that the Fed's and the IRS were continually evaluating.

We traveled north on Interstate-95 through New York for about twenty miles, north into a boat yard in Norwalk, Connecticut. It was obviously a pretty private high-end boat yard with a high chain link fencing around the perimeter, with barbed wire on top. Large expensive boats were at the docks and on land apparently for repairs, renovations, or storage. We went into a building that sold parts, oars, rowboats, some clothing, and tools. Additionally, there was a large boat garage that was attached to the store, where a yacht was being worked on by several men, which could be seen through an opening once inside the main store. Anthony had explained that he wanted me to "watch his back" because he was confronting a guy that owed him a lot of money that was loaned to him, and it was a few months since he had paid his vig.

This guy wasn't paying his vig, which meant repercussions. (The slang term *vig* came into use by mobsters, who made illegal loans with very high interest rates in order to finance questionable money needs.)

As we walked in, a man behind the counter, the owner and guy Anthony had loaned the money to, recognized Anthony. He immediately appeared to be concerned and frightened. He came directly around the counter with a forced smile on his heavily whiskered and dirty, greasy; face to shake our hands after wiping them off on a rag from his back pocket. Anthony never introduced me because I was no longer beside him. I was to watch his back, cover his moves and not know anything that was said or seen, should ANYONE ASK.

Anthony was not pleased, and directly asked, "Where's my money?" The guy tries to explain how business has prevented him from paying his debt in so many ways. But Anthony is not hearing any of it, because non-payment is always unacceptable. Everyone who borrows money from a shylark (or loan shark) must pay the vig (interest on the money) on the date and the amount agreed upon initially when agreeing to the loan. There are no excuses, just like when the bank loans out money. The collateral is in jeopardy when payment is NOT made which in this case: his collateral could be his ass on the line and could be his business.

Apparently, this guy, I later found out, needed the money for some stolen goods, which would benefit his business. He intended to turn the merchandise around for a large profit, but the process was thwarted due to delays caused by an inability to turn the merchandise as expected. So he had unwisely been holding back on payment for about two months while trying to dump the merchandise, typically to boat owners.

The guy was nearly crapping in his pants and sweat was running down his face from his forehead. He was visibly, physically showing complete fear when one of his men who was in the other room steps out between me and Anthony, and asks him what's wrong. Anthony's back is to the new guy, but Anthony doesn't turn knowing that I've got his back.

The owner doesn't answer, probably hoping that the entrance of another person/witness could be a safe distraction. Anthony, still without turning around, tells the guy, "Take a walk, it's none of your business."

The guy is stupid enough to say, "Maybe I'll make it my business." With that, Anthony gave a sideways glance at me as if to say, *you take care of this a-hole.*

I, however, was already in motion. The instant that this guy declared himself to be a hero, I grabbed an oar that was standing up against the wall next to me and drove it into the guy's chest so fast that he couldn't and didn't prepare himself. He was catapulted back into a rowboat that was on display, hitting his head on a seat but not knocking him out. I walked over in front of him, never taking my eyes off the entire room, and told him to just stay there and not to move. He stayed lying in the boat like a good doggie! Then the owner decided to *try to* call the police, can you believe it?! This would have been the dumbest move he ever made, if he were successful. Just as he gets to the pay phone located on the wall near me. I pushed him aside and ripped the phone out of the wall and handed it to him. He stood there with the torn-out phone hanging from his hands looking between me and Anthony, with absolute fear in his eyes and face, having no idea what to do next.

Anthony had not even moved during all of this. He slowly and decisively explained to this guy how it would be: he had better get all the money borrowed, along with the VIG owed for now three months, by the end of the week. Anthony said he didn't care where he got the money from; sell his cars, his house, or one of the boats outside, whatever it took. He explained where he would be and added that if he didn't comply there would be severe repercussions. And that I would be teaching the lessons for him along with some other competent teachers. The guy looks at me, then Anthony, and says okay. He stuck with the agreement and I never had to have any other dealings or communications with him after that day.

On the way home Anthony asked me how and why I decided to hit the guy with an oar. He was nearly laughing as he said it, and he looked at me while driving with a big smirk on his face. I told him that although I believed I could take the guy one on one with no problem, I didn't want to mess up the place, or my suit, with a brawl. I also believed that the remaining men in the boat garage saw the incident and decided to not intervene. I thought the oar would end the contest pretty fast, as it did. He cracked up laughing, and looked directly at me saying, "You just don't stop surprising me." Then he asked me why I didn't use my karate training. I explained that simply because there was an oar there, and I believe in ending a confrontation as easily and as soon as possible. My karate instructor once told me in the beginning of my training, when I was a white-belt beginner, that I was to win a fight by whatever means possible, and as quickly as possible.

Anthony thought that over for a moment, and then asked me, "Why?"

I told him about an experience I had in class when I was a beginner. There were very few white male students in the alternate class in NYC when I joined. In fact, I was often usually the only white boy in the class. My main class was in Scarsdale, NY, closer to my Rye trucking office, where I usually went. However, I was big, and I had plenty of fighting experience during my youth. So my instructor/sensei put me in what is called *kumite* (or free fighting) against black belts even though I was a white belt. He did that so that I didn't get too rambunctious and hurt someone by mistake, trying to use karate methods of fighting that I really had no proficiency in at that time. Our karate style was Japanese, and we fought without any pads, gloves, or facial protection, and it was full contact fighting. However, it was understood that we were not to try and hurt one another, but simply provide typical contact, while always trying to stay away from the opponent's face. We had specific strikes that I would still use today, because they are really difficult to protect one's self from. In the last hour of the typical four-hour training for that day, and we're then matched up against opponents to *kumite* (free fight). I'm put up against a black belt who was a second-degree black belt which pretty much means he can *kick my butt* blindfolded with both hands tied behind him, just coming out of sleeping. We start off sparring and he does a spinning back kick that is so fast I don't see it coming, and I also didn't even know what it was. Consequently, I'm kicked right in the side of my face which brings me to the ground on hands and knees. Although he was not supposed to do that kick to the face of an opponent who is a beginner, I shake it off and stand up. I'm ready to spar again when he does the exact same kick and, again, I go down. The sensei doesn't say a thing. I later find out because he believed that I could somehow defend myself and prevail. This second time the whole class laughed, making remarks about the big white boy being destroyed by their friend. That was until our instructor looked at them and they knew to shut up real fast or pay the consequences, which in general is an ass kicking from him. I was taught by two men who are two of the best in the entire world—that's a fact! They're both a seventh-degree black belt, which is only one degree under the master of our style, which is considered to be the fiercest of all styles, in any country.

So I shake it off again, quickly, because I don't take harassment too well and stand ready to spar. This guy tries it again!?! Now what happens next is only because he let his guard down by trying to show off to his friends how he can kick *the big white boy's* ass, with the same kick three times in a row. He challenges me with the words "How 'bout it, white boy?" without even changing kicks or style. When he did try it again, I was pretty pissed, and ready for him with every single fiber in my body. As he came around, I bent down and raised up my left arm, stopping his leg spin at the knee, and instantly coming up with my right fist into his groin and upper thigh as hard as I could which picked him up off the matt, landing him on his back. He was far better than me, but lots lighter. He was completely stunned, as he should have been, because there is no way I should have been able to do this to him, if he'd been focused. Well, I was on him like stink on shit. Knees on his chest as hard as I could, before he even realized it, and I punched him in the face at least twice which didn't put him out but slowed his actions. I then grabbed him by the collar of his Gi (fighting uniform) and belt and lifted him up to a level where I threw him upside down against the wall. He slid down with his head on the floor and legs over his head—knees on the mat, upside down. He was smaller than me in height and lots of weight, which in general shouldn't have meant anything at all because of his training. The two-minute fight bell rang which is what ends the match, and I stood back and waited for him to get up. When he did, we bowed to one another, bowed to our sensei and then our master (Mas Oyama), who's photo always hangs on the wall, and I started to sit down with the other students on the floor.

But Sensei called my name, and I know that it's because of my actions. I'm going to get an ass kicking by him in front of the class, and maybe thrown out of the training. I turn and walk over to him and respond, "Yes, sensei?"

He comes closer to me standing right in front of me, looks up (because he is about a foot or so shorter than me) and says, "I have one question for you."

I ask, "What is that, sensei?"

He says, "Wa took you so wong?"

I said I thought that I had to use only karate, when *dong kumite*. He told me, "You don't know karate yet, so you do whatever you have to do to win." Coming from a man who could take twenty of me at one time, I never forgot that day, that experience, or that advice. By the way, I earned some respect that day and was befriended by most every person in the class, over time. However, not everyone was on board with that, because those were the days of black panthers and lots of hatred of whites by blacks and blacks by whites.

By the time I had explained that whole occurrence to Anthony we were back at my car parked at the diner in Rye, NY, and I went back to my office to end the day there.

I'd always had a great sense of awareness, but in this line of work with the men that I had to deal with, I knew I had to take that awareness to another level. I needed to be keenly attuned to this environment at all times. Not just because of the possible danger by being involved with Anthony, but because there was always someone who you knew that really didn't like you, and would lie, cheat, steal, and do anything they could to destroy your name, your position, your integrity, so they could further themselves in some way. Rats in a cage!

Our lives were called "clandestine" for a reason. It was important to keep a low profile and keep as many people in the dark as possible within and outside of our own ranks.

Nicknames

Anthony called me at my office one day and told me to meet him at the restaurant downtown after work. I got there around 7:00 p.m. that evening and after a drink at the bar we went into the dining room and dined together. Anthony explained that he wanted to ask if I was interested in doing any "side work" for him. I asked him what kind of side work he had in mind, because I was not interested in taking lives. He laughed and said, "Do you think that I have anything to do with killing people?" I said, "Of course not, and I don't either… unless it was to protect myself or someone I loved or respected." The smile disappeared and he looked at me like he didn't know what to say, which was always bullshit with him, because Anthony always knew what to say! His approach is to use body language and/or facial expressions to see if a person will hang himself with his next words. I kept quiet and continued to eat. He asks me if I would be interested in helping him with his accounting, by collecting some money from time to time. He said he saw how I thought and acted and that I would be good at it and could make some decent extra money. I told him I'd definitely be interested, and that's when it began.

Then he asks me if I know how he got his nickname "Hickey" which I didn't, so he told me his story: He had grown up on a farm in upstate New York until he was a young teen. His family then moved to NYC where his peers gave him the nickname of "the Hick" because of his rural roots. He pretty much had to survive in the Big Apple like everyone who's under-privileged, and also new to the city. He had to fight, and win, and prove himself continually which quickly toughened him up to the city life. He was already strong from the daily work of farm life, but city living is a different kind of tough, especially since he was of Italian descent. At that time, due to all the crime, including bootlegging, most of the police were constantly down on the Italians. He also was brought to NYC because his grandfather was in the Mafia and got a job for his son, Anthony's father.

When he was old enough, he joined the army during World War II. In the fifties he was incarcerated for stealing a car, put on parole after two years in prison. In 1957, his sister was abducted by two black men and beaten up for not relenting to their unwanted sexual advances. In other words, they had tried to rape her, and she fought back, and then they beat her up, putting her in the hospital. When Anthony heard about this and visited his sister in the hospital, he found out that the police were doing nothing about it, probably because she was an Italian. So he went in search of the perpetrators. After a few days he was directed to them by his grandfather who was a "made man," known and respected in the city. When Anthony found them, he beat them both up with a baseball bat, putting THEM in the hospital. Consequently, the police arrested him and that's the second time he was put in prison this time for aggravated assault. But Anthony's family criminal lineage went way back, assuring that he was well established as an associate with Mafia crime families. He was incarcerated in Sing Sing prison for ten years.

Here is a side note concerning Anthony. While he was in prison, he went to the library nearly every day and studied law, among other things. He had a friend while in Sing Sing that was doing life for murder. Anthony studied his case and the law and brought his findings of the law concerning this guy's sentencing to an attorney, and the charges were dropped during another trial, and the man was released. I know this man and not only respected him but considered him a friend. Although he was of a Hebrew decent, he was a coveted associate with Anthony as long as they lived. It was a shame that Anthony was so intelligent but could only direct his thoughts and actions toward illegal means. I believe he was the smartest or should I say most intelligent man I have ever met.

After his nickname explanation, he asked me if I had ever been given a nickname. I told him that I was known as "the Indian," when I was in high school. He asked me why and I explained that it was given to me by a friend of mine named Sam Chiccorelli, who was matched up with me during a gym class, where we were to wrestle each other. Chick was on the wrestling team and I was not. He was kicking my butt on every move, and then he had me in a hold on the floor where he was stretched over my upper body, holding me down. We were friends but I didn't like this one bit, so I let out a scream; bench pressed him and threw him behind me. He was so stunned that his only reply was to just stand up. When I stood up, I turned and ran into him, grabbing him with my arm around his neck and my other arm through his legs. Picking him up, I ran with him screaming into the bleachers. Luckily, he was able to turn his body, so he didn't get hurt, and neither did I. That's when he yelled out that I was like a wild Indian and the hanger stayed with me throughout high school, especially when in bar fights in upstate New York.

Whenever I was involved in a fight at school or in a bar, everyone knew me as "the Indian." Interestingly enough, my great grandmother claimed that she was half Chippewa, so I actually could be part American Indian. Of course, my father was the role model for the TV show *All in the Family*, and my father was the prototype for the main character, Archie Bunker. His prejudice kept them from admitting that there was any Indian blood in the family. The fact is I have no idea if she was half Chippewa or not.

When Anthony stopped eating, he told me that he doesn't want *everyone* to know that he'll be calling me "The Indian." He explained that he'd seen others lose a lot of confidentiality when, too early in their involvement, too many people know their nickname or hanger as we put it. He suggested that my nickname be known only among his close associates. Then if he wanted me to do a certain thing for him, he could pass the message to me without everyone else knowing who it was. It was kept that way for ten years and not even my wife (his daughter) knew what he called me. He used to kid me by putting different hangers on me like, "Charlie the Hat," "Charlie the level," or just the "The Kid."

Anthony and His Attitude

I got this call one day in my office up in Westchester from Anthony. He asked me to meet him at the Empire State Building at nine o'clock the next morning. He said he had an appointment with a union leader (I'm definitely not using his name) about the problems that we'd been having with the local teamsters union. These problems were not only with our company, but others as well. Apparently, things were getting out of hand, or into his hand!

I'm standing at the street level of the building just outside of the entrance. When Anthony comes walking up the sidewalk in a custom-made black Tuxedo, with a top hat, black cane with a silver head, patent leather shoes, and light-blue tux shirt. Apparently, that was the only thing that he could put on from the night before, wherever he was. I never did get the reason for the tux. And I knew better than to ask. He liked his privacy! If he wanted me or anyone to know…he'd tell us himself.

We went inside and took the elevator to one of the upper floors to a first-class meeting room where we were to meet with this guy. There were four other men already there sitting at a twelve- or fourteen-foot table, two to each side and the head guy that we were to meet with was at the far end of the table. When we walked in everyone stood up and shook hands. Anthony knew everyone with exception of an attorney that was presumably associated to the unions. Anthony introduced me and said that I had firsthand experiences with the problems that we were having, because I was involved in management of more than one trucking outfit. Anthony sat at the other end of this table and I sat on the side. Anthony and this guy had a pretty lengthy conversation with occasional questions to me pertaining to what I knew and an occasional remark from some others. But it was primarily between Anthony and this union leader. I could see that things were not going the way that Anthony wanted and I could tell by his reactions and his leg shaking under the table (just like they did when I told him his daughter was pregnant, years ago) that he was about to explode. Everyone at the meeting was aware that things were getting out of hand. So Anthony took hold of the situation in his way.

Suddenly! Anthony shoves the table away from him and it tips the union leaders chair back against the wall, while the table pins his neck against the wall. All that is above the table is his head pinned against the wall and his hands on the end of the table to hold himself up, while his body weight is pulling down on his head. I nearly lost it but knew better. Everyone who was there jumped up and stood back while Anthony very calmly explained exactly what he wanted. He told this guy exactly what he expected and that was that.

After he's completed his thoughts, Anthony pulled the table back and got up from his chair. He calmly walks over the guy who is still leaning back against the wall because his chair is leaning so far back, he can't right it. Anthony walked up to him and gently pulled the chair back on its legs. The guy struggled to stand so Anthony grabbed his arm very gently and helped him up. He grabs the guys hand and shakes it while he says his good byes. He tells him he'll be in touch, and we leave. Everyone else just stands there in complete amazement, awe, respect, and complete and total fear.

We went down to the street together and he said why don't I come over to the house this weekend and help him with some painting he wants to get done, never mentioning what had occurred upstairs. It's like I am just supposed to accept and expect whatever happens when I'm with him. And I had learned to do exactly that. We parted and when I got to my car, I must have laughed for ten minutes. I'll never forget the scene with this guy's head pinned against the wall by the table. From what I had learned later is that this guy was somehow in charge of all the union locals. He was the big fish with unions. I know it wasn't Fitzsimmons who took over Jimmy Hoffa's position, however, he may have somehow been even more powerful.

That was a Friday and I remember that because my wife and I went over to Anthony's the next day and went swimming and had a barbeque for dinner. When it was later in the day he and I went into his den and talked about a bunch of issues that needed to be discussed. His den was just like the rest of the house. It's decorated in very expensive furnishing including a couch, chairs, TV cabinet, paintings, drapes with valance, doors to the patio, wallpapered walls, and an electric fireplace. We were talking by the warm fireplace, smoking cigars and drinking very expensive brandy in a snifter.

One of the truths that is learned on the street (and in life only most people ignore it) is that if a poor man steels a wallet or even a car, he is called a thief. However, if a rich man steals a company or an idea that was someone else's, he is building empires.

The poor man is reviled and punished according to his crime in years of prison and the rich man is respected and revered, for what he has achieved. It appears that the more that you steal the less you have to fear especially if you have the cash to prevent the punishment. In NYC the local cops were bribed to allow certain areas of crime to persist. If the crime or infringement was larger than the payoff or bribe, it had to go up the ladder of authority such as a police captain, judge, or even a senator. Whatever it took, as long as there was a profit, which allowed an acceptable result for getting it.

We were discussing our problems with the unions and their demands for an increase in hourly pay for the men, and also for increasing the numbers of drivers. I have no idea what the profits are in the trucking companies, because my job is to just increase the profits not to count other people's money. What I do know is that I'm respected in the industry because my outfits are making profits. But out of the blue, I threw out a convoluted idea that I had been thinking about and shared it with Anthony.

I explained the problem was that the unions always want more money for the men without a guarantee that the men will increase or even maintain their production. In fact, the union delegates are constantly trying to slow the work down so that the companies will be forced to hire more men. I asked, "Why don't we have some sort of reward system for the drivers and dock men, where it benefits both them and us?" He looks at me like "wow" you're going to surprise me again, and says, "Like what?" I asked if we could give the men an hourly increase but have guidelines they had to comply with before they could receive the increase.

He said, "That sounds like a good idea, but how do we do it?" I suggested that the men get an increase per hour but couldn't get it until they were with us for a certain amount of time like five years. This would show that they were interested in not only being union men, but also being company men. Anthony pours us some more brandy as he is running this over in his mind.

Anthony was quiet, thinking, and then picked up the phone and dialed a number. His phone is in a stylish wooden case that has a top on hinges with seashells imbedded in the wood. The guy answered, and I have no idea who he has called. But when I heard what he was about to say, I thought of the guy with his head pinned to the wall with the table. He says with a very determined voice, "If one piece of freight moves in this country by air, you're a dead man." Then he just hangs up and resumes sitting on the couch drinking his brandy and smoking his cigar.

He says this on his home phone! We never say anything that can be used against us on the phone, because our phones are tapped twenty-four, seven. I nearly lost it, but again knew better. I'm not sure of the time or even the year that this occurred, somewhere around 1971 or 1972. What I do know is that there was a period of time where NO airfreight moved in this country, because of that phone call made in his den. That's a fact that can be found on the internet, somehow. I'm now seventy-two years old and although I'm pretty capable, I can't keep up with the increasing and complicated updates in technology.

What I also later realize is that my suggestion sparked in his brain. My suggestion came from a management position of trying to increase production and somehow satisfy the unions. His mind takes that to a whole other dimension, of course. His mind thinks in terms of not necessarily honest dimensions. What he sees is that the men are to get additional hourly pay (later determined) of one dollar per hour that will be put into a bank for the employee. And as I suggested, the union member can later receive the money when he leaves our employ. But he must first stay in our employ for a minimum of five years before he is eligible for it. If the employee leaves prior to the five-year mark, the money reverts back to the company. And the clincher is that the whole time that the employee's potential future money is waiting in the bank, the interest is banked to the company (Anthony and others) instead of going to the employee. That interest would soon turn into millions of dollars for the company. This worked for years, until the government got hold of it and, from what I understand, some attorney took the heat and went to prison because of my idea and Anthony's decision.

However, it was not my decision or intension to have the interest go into the company's hands. That's what the attorney who put together the deal that I originally shared went to the joint for. I didn't suggest taking money that wasn't ours, I just wanted to find a way to end the trucking problems with the union.

After the barbeque, Anthony and I went back in his den to, I thought, relax. I guess he was still amped up by the phone call and new plan, so he enthusiastically said, "Let's paint this place! I want to change the color of the ceiling."

We got the paint from the garage and we began preparing by covering all the furniture which we'd pulled to the middle of the room. We covered the carpeting and all that needed to be protected. We started painting the ceiling. He was on a ladder and I could roll and brush the ceiling from the floor due to my height. I can touch over eight feet high so I don't need a ladder, especially with a paintbrush or roller in my hand. We were talking and listening to music while were painting, and he lets out this very loud fart. The next thing I know is that it was also an unbelievably foul-smelling fart. I said to him, "Do me a favor, and if you have to fart, go outside because it's really gross."

He says to me, "Hey, there are people who would pay me to help me paint and smell my farts just so that they could be with me."

I walked over to him and handed him my paintbrush and told him, "Here get someone to help you paint, so you can make some money. I'm going home." I got my wife and little boy and went home.

I don't think that anyone ever had the nerve to do something like that to him. He didn't even say anything when I left. I think he was totally flabbergasted. We went over to his house the next day and I continued helping him with the painting. And we finished it with no farting. The only thing that he said to me was, "As usual, Charlie, you don't stop surprising me."

After we had finished the painting and cleaned up, we were putting things away in the garage when he looked across the street and saw that there were two men sitting in a car. It was obvious that they were Fed's. He walked across the street and said to the two men that he would be leaving in a couple of hours and going downtown. If they wanted to go and get some dinner, he wouldn't be leaving for at least three to four hours. Then he walked back to the garage with a big smile on his face and we went inside. When we left to go home later in the evening, he left for Manhattan and waved at the agents in the car to come and follow him.

That's how Anthony operated. Catch me if you can!

The FBI Now and Then and the Ballplayer and Balls

Because I was associated to the Genovese family through my father-in-law, I was looked upon by the FBI as a criminal. In the beginning I wasn't a criminal, only a trucking terminal manager, but that didn't matter to them. My telephone was always tapped. I could hear the clicks and the slight tones when I picked up the phone to answer it or make a call. To my knowledge there was no need for a judge to give a warrant, they did what they needed to do, and that was that. Back then they didn't have to get permission.

What I used to do when on the phone, because I didn't and still don't like my personal space invaded, was to try and insult anyone who was listening and wasn't supposed to be. Let's say I'm talking to a guy named Tommy. I'd say things like. Hey, Tommy, did you know that the reason this phone is tapped, and some scumbag FBI person is listening is because I screwed his mother, or his sister, or his wife? It didn't matter. And I know that it really didn't hit home with them, because they knew I was just trying to get their goat, knowing they were listening. It just was a method of letting them know that we knew all the phones were tapped, so don't expect anything that would help you get evidence against anyone. There are all kinds of things we used to say to let them know we knew they were listening. None of it mattered, other than if and when they could be in on taking us down, it would be more fun for them. But at the time it was fun for us, just to let them know that we knew they were listening.

Later when I was more involved, nobody said anything on a private phone anyway. So they were wasting their time listening as much as they were. We didn't ever say if we were meeting at a certain place.

We'd use codes, like…hey, I'll meet ya over at that bus stop. Meaning a café or diner we had met at once or twice before. If it was at one of our regular meeting places, we would never even say we were going to meet. We'd just say something like, "I'm on my way home so I can get a good meal." That meant…meet me at our favorite restaurant, because they had the best Italian food in NYC. Now you're thinking that when they followed us then they would know what that meant. Wrong! We knew what was being said in code because we knew one another. We didn't use the same codes, just knew. Usually, it was something that had been discussed at another time that gave us the hint. It sounds complicated, but at the time, it was necessary to survive, or should I say keep ahead of the Feds.

Now I went through all this to explain what I was talking about before concerning knowing what someone was saying about a meeting without saying where. When Anthony asked me to meet him so we could go to see the guy who hadn't been paying his debt, he knew what had happened that day and said to me something like, "I must leave now, and whatever you do, don't let anyone swap jewelry on you or you'll have to go and punch him in the café again." That meant, in code, "I'll meet you in Port Chester!" He met me there and no one followed either of us.

But then again, they often DID follow us, so it really didn't make too much of a difference. The real objectives were to not use our phones and use codes whenever necessary or possible.

These are the times when not only could they listen in on your phone conversations, but they bugged places including your home, office, or a restaurant that you might regularly attend.

I've mentioned that we had one restaurant where we knew we were safe to discuss anything. That was because it was owned by brothers who were "made" men and Anthony may have had a piece of it to boot. They had the place screened regularly for any bugs. Everyone who worked there knew the score. They all knew who was associated and treated them like monarchs. There were lots of reasons for that, especially because they were paid better than anyone else in their business and were tipped a hell of a lot more by guys who used other men's money.

We ate at the dining room tables with all the other patrons who believed that it was one of the best Italian restaurants in town. Also, many patrons knew that it was owned by made brothers. They also knew that it was attended by lots of other made or connected or just associated men. It was like dining with Al Capone in the old days in Chicago. You could tell that they loved not only the food but the company. You could see the excitement when someone like Anthony walked in to have a meal. Everyone was always very polite and cordial when it came to others in the dining room. This was especially true of Anthony and men like him!

The restaurant's bar was a little more private. It was where I was to be killed, but that's a story for later in this writing. There usually were just persons who were associated in there, with an occasional acquaintance sharing drinks. Sometimes, however, there were people of, what one would call, stature. I didn't revere anyone that way. I couldn't give a crap who someone was, and never did, and still don't, when it comes to their money, association or business. I always showed respect to everyone and still do, to all alike. But I never did and still don't feel elated to meet some dignitary, celebrity or billionaire. I loved to see successes, so good for them! Afterall, it's part of the American dream. And I've always loved America, for one could strive for something greater because of our freedom and opportunity to do so.

After I was able to "escape from New York," as I often say, I became a commercial construction superintendent who built banks, restaurants, subterranean parking structures, shopping malls, condos, and midrise buildings. After that I was a California licensed contractor which allowed me to construct up to a ten-story building. I then designed and constructed custom homes in an unbelievably beautiful area called Lake Tahoe, CA. I mention this because although I never had a formal education, I was still able to not only survive but excel because of living in the greatest country in the world, The United States of America. Never forget that you, too, have the same opportunities, just "never back up" and believe in yourself. My change in life from a criminal to be moral, law-abiding citizen will be explained in another chapter later in this book.

After all of this…back to the restaurant. There was a famous baseball player that used to come to the restaurant and into the bar. Everyone knew him because he was a big deal in baseball. First thing is, I didn't watch or even know anyone in baseball, football, hockey, soccer, basketball or any other professional game. When I was young, kids at school had their baseball cards that they used to exchange and brag about. I never had the money to waste on them, and they were never given to me. I never watched professional anything, because we were not allowed to watch TV during the day, unless it was raining. We were out playing ball or in my case usually doing some work that my father had for me to do, around the property. It wasn't often that my father watched any sports, so neither did we.

And my father liked things like Gunsmoke, and the Lone Ranger as much as I did. When I left home at the age of fourteen, I still was not into nor could I have been into any sports. Unless it was a football game on TV during Thanksgiving or the Super Bowl. I'm still that way to this day. Consequently, I never even tried to be friends with his greatness, like the others around him in the bar.

This baseball star used to move from one wise guy to the next opening his suit coat and giving them "illegal" Cuban cigars, in the outward effort to try and impress them more. The fact is that they put up with him, but no one I was close to really thought much of him. Other than hearing that he was a great baseball player, I really don't remember his name or position and I still don't care.

But one evening I was standing there at the side of the bar and this guy's gorgeous wife comes over to talk to me. I'm most often the youngest guy there, I'm considered to be handsome, and so apparently I may be an interest to her. I was at the end of the bar near the entrance so I could see everything that was happening and am typically concerned for my own protection. She was very pretty, no actually beautiful, and about ten or so years older than me, which put her in her thirties. That was usually an attraction to me. She came and stood next to me because I never sat at a bar. I always stood while in a bar, and even in this place which is as safe as it comes, if I was in good graces with the rest of my associates. I'm still that way to this day. I typically don't sit down when in crowds, and I used to only sit in a position with my back to the wall, so I can see everything that is going on in a restaurant.

She began asking me about what I did for a living. I told her I was a trucking terminal manager and explained some of my experiences as she smiled, listening like she really cared. Then out of the blue, she moves closer and puts her hand on my stomach. She feels a gun in my belt, and I think it turns her on, a lot. We keep talking and I move the gun around to the other side away from her hand. Now she's smiling at me and asks me if I think she's pretty. She knows she's freaking beautiful! I tell her very, and that she's also very sexy. That's when she puts her hand down my pants and grabs my testicles.

We were on the side of the bar so that I can see everyone, and her husband was in front of the bar, with his back to the bar, talking to several men. He was laughing and having a good old time, while his wife had my nuts in her hand, playing with them, while we were talking. Thing is, I knew better. I'd like to tell her to meet me some time and go to a hotel and have a good time. But since her husband is, for some reason, accepted by all these guys, I can't, wouldn't and didn't do anything. I tried to explain my position to her out of respect for my associates and friends…not her husband. I explained that I have a code that I won't have sex with any of the men's wives that I'm associated with. I told her that as far as her husband went, I thought he was a mutt, and didn't impress me in any way. But because he's accepted here with these men, I have an obligation to stay away from her, period.

She's still playing around with my nuts when she's called by her husband and must break away. As she's leaving and has pulled her hand out of my pants she said, "Too bad, because I think we would have had a great time!" And believe me, I knew it also. For some reason I couldn't stick around.

As I'm leaving, Anthony pulls me aside and says, "You are f———ing nuts, you know that?" Not the first time he's said that to me, for sure. I play stupid and ask why do you say that? He's nearly laughing the whole time. He explained, because I would have had to have either put "whatever his name was" in the hospital or kill him if he had seen what Anthony had seen. I said, with a straight face, I didn't know what he was talking about. So he asked if I was going to meet her some time. I asked him, "Is she married to someone in there?"

He said, "You know who she's married to."

I said, "If she's married to someone in there, which is associated with you and your friends, I'd never do that." Then I added, "Even though I think that guy is an asshole." He let out a laugh and said, "That's exactly what I thought. You're always a standup guy, even when the temptation is that great." "Truth is," he says, "I'm not sure that I'd have walked away. What a babe!" I respond with, "Thanks a lot, now I think I'll go out and shoot myself." He left me, and off I went, back home to my own beautiful wife.

The bottom line is that I never did and still don't have any athlete, movie star, singer, band, or whoever as a revered model in my life. I've only had three heroes in my life, until reading a biography about the fourth. My first was and is Audie Murphy (if you don't know who he is look him up). Then there is Mother Teresa and Cory Ten Boom. I also should mention that I have a real deep respect and appreciation for Winston Churchill. The stars do their job and I do mine. These other four are beyond understanding as men and women. There were some movie stars, athletes, and amazing singers that I got to sit down with and have a meal, or a glass of champagne with people like Frank Sinatra and some others at the Copa Cabana. Sinatra was a great guy and very nice to be around, but that was that!

Back to the FBI. One day I was downtown walking on the sidewalk after parking my car. I was on my way to meet with MM on some business. I had a favor to ask of him concerning a family member and a union matter. He had a meeting downtown, so we were to meet near where he was having his meeting with someone else.

Now, as I'm just walking along the sidewalk minding my own business thinking about how I was to present this request to him, I suddenly see two guys walking across the street toward me. I could tell by their Thom McCann shoes and wrinkled shelf-bought suits, which didn't fit them correctly, that they were cops, or detectives, or likely FBI agents. I kept on walking trying to seem like I hadn't noticed them. But when they got about six feet away, they ran toward me and pushed me against a brick wall, banging my head. My first reaction and my second and third was to protect myself and beat the shit out of anyone who would do that, especially since they didn't declare that they were cops of any kind or FBI agents. Now I really didn't know who they were. Maybe this was due to something that I had done, and they were paid to take me out, or just beat the crap out of me. I came off the wall and broke the first guys nose with my upward thrust of the heel of my palm. He was out for the count and holding his nose, while the second guy was pummeling me with his fists. I kept my face clear of his aggression with my forearm, and then spun around to position myself for protection and defense and beat the snot out of the second guy. I used my knife hand to his neck, after punching him in the solar plexus, and he started to go down. When suddenly, I was out! Apparently a third agent came in from behind and used the butt of his gun on my skull to put me out of the disagreement.

Please understand this! At the time of this writing I have the utmost respect for any law officer. I also believe that whatever they did back then is now perfectly okay with me. They put their lives online every day, back then and today.

I came to consciousness, tied to a chair with a bright lite in my eyes, completely blinding my sight. I had no idea as to where I was or who was there. Understand this is NYC, in the nineteen seventies and things happened back then, everybody would just turn away as if nothing was going on. This brings to mind how a woman in Brooklyn was screaming for help as she was being beaten, raped, and stabbed to death, but no one came to her aid! People admitted that they heard her continued screams for help but didn't even call the police much less try to help. If I was there at that time, I know that I would have intervened. I know because I have done it more than once when it comes to women being physically abused by some nasty man.

Back to the street fight with the Feds. I'm just getting to the fun part! When I woke up, I heard a voice that asked me why I was on that street and who was I meeting with. Then without even a chance to answer (and there was no way that I would have) this person asked me what we were up to? "Duh! Are ending you f——ing kidding me?" Did he think for one second that I was about to answer him? I sat there and he told me I'd better answer if I knew what was good for me. I finally realize where I was and who was doing the asking. Then I said, "Have I seen you in the movies, because you remind me of someone. I can't see you, but you sound just like that asshole that I'm trying to remember. He was a big, ugly, real dumb f——, who is also a total pussy, ties down someone before hitting him, so he doesn't get his ass kicked."

Oops, bad move! The next thing that I partially see is a fist blocking the light coming toward my face. I always have had, and still do at the age of seventy-two, a good reflex action. I was able to turn my head in a split second before getting a fist in my face. Consequently, I got a fist in the side of my head instead. That was a good move! But actually, they weren't stupid. They knew that if they hit a guy in the nose it could kill him by driving his nose membrane into his brain. So he asked me again. Who was I meeting and why? I said wait one minute, I can't think after being punched in the head. That bought me about thirty seconds before I was asked the same question with a little more aggressiveness. Well, I had to answer with something. So I said, "I was meeting your wife and we were going to get a room to have some sex together." Actually, I explained it with much different wording. Guess what? Here comes mister big fist from the other side. Again, I was able to turn my head at the very last split second and got the hit on the side of my forehead. I have never had my nose broken to this day. Even Michael M. never broke my nose, and I still think of him as the toughest guy I ever came against way back in grammar school. I can still hear him saying, "After school, Elwyn."

I was really glad that I was not carrying a weapon, or I would have been put in jail after a beating.

Well, a few more slaps, a few more punches, and a few more questions, and they decided that I was a pain in the ass, in general. So along with a few curses, a few warnings, a few promises, I was untied. Then, I was pretty much thrown out of the downtown police station.

After I hit the ground and rolled into a standing position, I asked them, "So whose wife was it?" Then I walked away and found my car, now several blocks away. I missed my meeting with MM, but we met the next day, when I found him in the restaurant and explained the situation, he cracked up when I explained what had happened and what my response to them was. The bottom line is that nothing that went on that day with them meant anything. MM helped me with my favor and that was just another day in the life that we lived.

I have to crack up when I think or see on TV how people react toward the police that are no way as violent today as back then but now, they are calling it "police brutality." Hell, maybe we should take away their guns like they do in England and let them run for their lives away from criminals who have guns. What the cops and the Feds used to do to us as I shared above was somewhat expected. Expected you say? Yup! WE WERE CRIMINALS, WHO HUNG AROUND WITH CRIMINALS! The police and the FBI put their lives on the line every single day they go out there on the street to protect us, and all I ever hear is complaints. If a few more criminals would be treated the way that we were back then, I'll bet a bunch that there would be a lot less criminals. They abuse the system and have some scumbag lawyer defend what they did. Have I gotten off? Yup…same reason! Scumbag lawyer! Another thing that you the reader should understand and share with others, is that these nitwit politicians who continually want to take guns from all citizens have no idea what would happen afterwards. I can personally assure you that then only the criminals, the gangs, the low life scumbags that definitely shouldn't, WILL be able to get them. And by the way, our constitutions second amendment allows us to have guns. Oh, and another issue is that most of the actresses and actors and politicians have bodyguards who are allowed to have weapons to defend them. Are they better than you or me? Forgetaboutit!

Let's get on to another issue but still on this page so to speak. The issue of the FBI following us around with helicopters. We'd be driving along a road or a highway and suddenly, realized that there was a helicopter following us. We would be having a family day with the kids and others. No one else, just family and there would be helicopters staggering over the rear yard, very obviously looking down on us with cameras, binoculars, sound devices, who knows what they had. Also, often a car with two agents sitting in the front would be parked outside the house. What we did know was that they weren't there because they ran out of gas. They weren't invading our privacy as would be claimed today. They were doing the job of trying to prevent crimes by watching known criminals.

Anthony had a beautiful house with a large in-ground swimming pool. We would spend a lot of time during the summers, in the pool and having family barbeque parties. I can't think of too many times that we had anyone except family. Yet there would be the helicopters, just hanging around, circling above. It got so that it was expected, and we didn't even pay them any mind. Anthony was away (in prison) for most of my life during those days. He was either in the joint, on the lam, or living in another country under political asylum. But there they were, flying overhead. I have always been a good artist. I'd won contests in school and still paint today when I have time. I designed the logo for one of our trucking companies and pretty much always liked to draw. I wanted to drain the pool and clean it out completely so that I could paint a fist with the middle finger sticking out on the bottom of the pool. So that when the Fed's flew over, they would see us giving them the finger. My mother-in-law wouldn't allow it for all the obvious reasons, such as kids, friends, and her own good taste. She was not only a physically beautiful woman, but also a very private and law-abiding one. It sure would have been fun to do it back then, though.

Recent news showed "Stingrays" technology for FBI aerial photography surveillance planes over cities which triangulates without a search warrant in order to locate the source of cell phone positions. In my time they used to use helicopters to locate and watch criminals. All the time! And, rightly SO!

The public today says that a little helicopter is invading on their privacy. But a big one didn't and doesn't. So why is it that there a lot of things that are considered an invasion of privacy, but an automobile following you is not? Hey, get this, if it's not too hard for your brain, because you may be a criminal yourself or know one! If you're a criminal you should have no rights that prevent the law from finding you, preventing you from doing something, and putting your sorry ass away, or back then, my own sorry ass.

Decades have passed, and I'm a changed man in many ways. That will be explained in a later chapter. Although I want to share how I feel about the police today, actually for a long time since I left that life of associations with criminals. I support our police, FBI, CIA, ICE, and any other organization that has men and women who are putting their lives on the line to protect and serve the citizens of the United States of America. When I am driving, and I see a policeman has pulled over a car and is walking toward it, I always slow down to see if for any reason that officer would need my assistance. I was wrong in the way that I lived back then and the attitude I had for the police. However, things were also different back then in other ways. For instance, how not only a lot of the police, but many of the judicial, and political lawmakers were paid off, so that the criminals could do what they wanted without ramifications. I'm not saying that things like that still don't go on today. I am saying that it is nowhere as common or as accepted as it was back then. I remember that I accepted the fact of my involvement in criminal actions partly because of this situation back then. Back then I considered myself as less of a criminal than the law enforcement officers and agencies that were taking bribes and thinking that they were not doing a criminal activity. Or if they did? Then they were thinking exactly like the criminals that were paying them off, in my opinion, or worse!

Decisions, Decisions, Decisions

I was leaving a downtown restaurant one evening after meeting with Anthony and some other men concerning some union problems. After leaving the restaurant I walked past the corner of the building on my way to my car, when I felt the cold muzzle of a pistol put against the side of my neck. I stopped walking and immediately heard a voice that I recognized that said, "How does it feel knowing you are about to die?" The voice was very shaky and somewhat highly pitched which made me think that the guy holding the gun was more afraid than I was. I had recognized the voice being from a guy that I had to collect money from because he neglected to pay back the loan or the vig owed.

The loan was made with a guy I'll call Tommy who was a loan shark to an acquaintance of his. He borrowed the money to purchase a truckload of stolen Scotch that he intended to resell for a sizable profit. He knew the guy that had the stolen booze in a warehouse ready to sell to him. When this guy, "Jimmy" met with the guy in a bar, he ignorantly, "no stupidly," paid him and went directly to the warehouse with a rented truck where the booze was supposed to be. But it wasn't there. Neither was the guy he had just paid who was supposed to meet him there. Apparently, the guy had already sold the load to someone else. After taking Jimmy's cash along with the prior sale cash, then he flew the coup never to be seen or heard from again.

Jimmy knew he couldn't go to Tommy and explain his stupid mistake of giving the guy the cash without seeing the booze and being able to take possession and load it right then. The transaction of borrowing the money was not dependent upon Jimmy getting the load of stolen booze, although the lender always knows what the money was loaned for. Just like in a bank! They loan you money because they assess what it is for and what the value is, so that they get back the money loaned. Jimmy still owed the money and the weekly vig until the entire amount was paid back in full. Borrowing money from a loan shark, also known as a shylark, is just like borrowing from a bank. You agree to the term, get the money, and pay it back. The bank doesn't care if you lost the money due to some stupid mistake. You still owe the money and the interest or vig (in loan shark or skylark terms) until the borrowed money is paid back, just like with a bank loan. Loan sharks use the term "vig" because if they were heard saying "interest" by the cops, it would be a reason to arrest them for being an unregistered or unapproved loan service. So after a couple of months Tommy hired me to find Jimmy and get his loan back.

Jimmy wasn't hard to find after I put the word out to a few bars that he used to patronize that I needed to talk with him. Owners of bars and bartenders in NYC knew to cooperate with issues like this which in general gave them limited protection. I found him up in northern Westchester County working for a building contractor as a carpenter laborer in a new development. He asked his boss if he could take a break to talk with me, and we were to meet in a park down the road. I trusted him but he never showed up! The search was on again. He was separated from his wife and also needed the money for his back-alimony payments. He was now apparently on the run with my knowledge that he had two kids that lived with his wife in Queens.

I put the word out again only with a little more obvious desire to find him, so typically a type of reward is offered for assistance in finding a guy on the run. There were some that would warn the guy. And there was a guy who wanted to get on the good side of the bad guys by ratting on the poor smuck that is hiding from the bad guys. I got notice from a bartender that Jimmy was working now at a warehouse in Jamaica, Queens. I went directly to the warehouse and waited for him to go to his car parked in an adjacent alley. He didn't see me until it was too late. I felt some compassion for the guy and wanted to talk to him, not hurt him. He didn't give me a chance.

When he saw me he reached inside his coat pocket and pulled out a .38 snub-nose pistol, immediately pointing it at me. I was only about six feet away and rushed him taking away the pistol while doing so, accidentally spraining his wrist in the process. At the same time, he started punching me and refused to listen, so I hit him in the face breaking his nose and put him on the ground. I didn't go any further although I could and should have. While he was on the ground trying stop the bleeding from his nose with his only good hand. I read him the riot act and told him he had better get the money up and delivered to me within a week, or he would have more than one broken bone. I thought that I had been very lenient on him because of the park issue, pulling a gun on me, and trying to hit me when I hadn't put a hand on him.

Well, apparently, he was unable to get the money up, so he decided to kill me instead as I came out of the restaurant. I asked him if he had the money, and he yelled NO! I told him that he had two options. One was to kill me, insuring he would be found and taken care of by the guys I just left. Or he could put the gun down and go find a way to repay Tommy, because it was him that was really pissed at Jimmy. I told him that if he put the gun away and just left, I would not go after him for his action of putting a gun to my head. He asked, "How can I believe you?" I told him, "Because I said it and I always keep my word, and I just want you to even up with Tommy."

I had found out that his wrist wasn't sprained but broken by accident when I took his gun away the first time. I also reminded him that I was about six feet away then and got the gun away from him. Did he think that I couldn't take his gun away right now? "So lower the gun and leave, before I take the gun or you die very soon for killing me."

I also told him that I wasn't afraid of dying, which is why I could do some things that I had done and would do later. I wasn't afraid of dying because of what my father used to preach to us often at the dinner table when he was there. He told us that hell is on Earth, because of all the pain, sorrow, misery that we go through while living here on earth. And heaven is when you die, because there is nothing, just a body in the ground decaying away until there is nothing. I believed his interpretation of life, so I didn't care if I lived or died.

I realized that Jimmy was in a bind way over his head. Also, that he made another dumb mistake because he and I knew he wasn't a guy who could murder someone. Also, he realized he had nowhere to hide. I then told him either shoot me or get the F out of here and get the money to me before I resumed looking for him, and he wouldn't like that. He left, and I held up to my word and didn't go after him for that incident.

One week later he told me, when he brought me the borrowed money and vig that he owed that he was able to speak to his wife concerning his mistakes. They were back together, and she had agreed to take out a second loan on their house to get the money for him to pay back his loan from Tommy. I was glad because he wasn't a bad guy, or a wise guy, just a guy trying to get even with a debt. I never, with exception of the drug dealer, wanted to hurt people unless they attempted to hurt me.

Oh yeah, there were a couple of incidents where two men had to be put in the hospital because they hurt my sister each in different ways. That's family business so I won't go further. But both got a severe beating when the opportunity arose, because of their actions.

Another family incident occurred because of my father. As you already know, I never got along with my father, but he was family and this situation needed to be taken care of. My father was in his eighties and he lived in upstate NY in a small town called Lake Clear, which is about forty miles from the Canadian border. He lived in a double wide that he had remodeled since he was a contractor and very good carpenter. He lived alone because he and my mother had separated when she finally caught him with another woman. They owned and operated a well-known Inn called Charlies Inn in Lake Clear Junction, NY until they separated. My mother never divorced him because she loved him till the day he died, and then she decided to give up her life on her own free will and died two weeks after he died. Both at the age of eighty-seven years old. She was a Proverbs 31 wife and mother.

My father's house was located at the end of a road that went to his property which had been subdivided from the acreage of Charlies Inn when they sold it. It was alone in the woods. One day, a neighbor who was a lot younger than my father, and older than me, knocked on his door. When my father answered the door there was some kind of a quarrel and the neighbor smashed my father in the face with the entry door. As I was told, he then threw my father off the patio onto the ground. My father never pressed charges and he never told me what happened. My sister told me after this had happened while I was living in Lake Tahoe, CA.

It was a couple of years later that the family was visiting my father and we were all at Charlies Inn playing pool and having fun together. For some reason I walked back to my father's house by the roadways instead of just crossing over Charlies Inn property to get to my fathers at the far end of the property. I cut across to the road that went to my father's house from the main road and was coming out of the woods when I saw the guy who had beat up my dad. He was going back into his house while his wife and kids were driving away in their car. Well, back then I had a hard time forgiving people and I decided to pay this Mutt back. I went to his house and knocked on his door, surmising that he was alone. When he came to the door, he opened it and asked what I wanted. He didn't know me, so he had no idea what was going to happen.

I told him very calmly who I was and asked him if it felt good to beat up an old man. He started to answer with an attitude when I grabbed him by the shirt collar and broke his nose with my other fist. I then hit him, knocking all of the air out of his lungs, and threw him off his stoop and onto the ground. I jumped on him and grabbed him by the neck with one hand strangling him. And with the other put my thumb into the corner of his eye where the eye is close to his nose. He started to try and hit me, when I explained that if he continued, I would pull his eye out of its socket, at the same time pushing on that area of his eye which will cause the eye to pop out of its socket. I learned this method in karate and had used it once on a guy who came up behind me and put me in a headlock. Not only could I not get out of his hold, but I couldn't breathe and thought I was possibly going to be killed. At that time this procedure was the only thing I could think of to get out of his hold. He had his eye put back in when they brought him to the hospital. I have no idea what the results were and honestly didn't care. He not only started the fight but did it in a cowardly way, by grabbing me from behind.

This neighbor of my father stopped trying to fight me because he realized that he might lose his eye. I then explained why he was getting this beating. I warned him that he had better not go near my father again, and if he called the police and I was arrested, he would find himself wide awake in a lake with cement blocks tied to his legs trying to breathe under water. I explained who I was associated with and that he would never be able to testify against me, because they would never find his dead worthless body. And that all of it would happen when I was incarcerated. I then gave him a backhand across his face, got up and walked to my fathers to get something out of my car before returning to where my family was.

I never heard word about this, so the warning worked. I never told anyone in my family about this until now. And that's only if they read this book.

Anthony's Arraignment and charges

Anthony DiLorenzo, who is reputed to be the heir-apparent to the Vito Genovese family of the Mafia, was indicted in 1972 in New York, by a Federal grand jury on charges of conspiring to transport $1 million worth of stolen International Business Machines stocks across state lines.

In 1972 "Hickey" had obtained a million dollars' worth of IBM CDs (open without a signature or owner) securities. Of course, we knew they had fallen off a truck as he was riding by. Well "Hickey" had one of his men, "Jackie the nose," drive the CDs out to a large construction site located in Pennsylvania to sell to the contractor there. The problem was that "Jackie the nose" was always a very flamboyant, well-dressed man who had women hanging on him like ornaments on a Christmas tree. He decided to take his new cherry-red Cadillac convertible with TWO beautiful blonds in the front seat with him.

Consequently, just about every construction worker on the commercial work site noticed him, his car and the women with him. I don't know how the takedown originated, but the FBI caught wind and put the pinch on the contractor who gave up Jackie. So "Hickey" sends Jackie on the lamb (in hiding) to California, because there are no extradition rights between New York and California, and at that time Jackie was wanted for the theft of the securities, not the transfer which is then considered a federal crime. Jackie had a hard problem staying out of town as instructed, and within a year he returned to NYC, unauthorized and against instructions, and is pinched within the hour.

Now I can't state that Jackie gave up Anthony. But it wasn't long after he was arrested that they arrested Anthony for the theft and transportation of the CD's, across state lines, which then makes it a federal crime. Jackie, I was told by Anthony, disappeared after that, and no one knew where he went, until they heard that he went across the river to new Jersey and was now the driver for John Gotti. That's only what I was told by Anthony, so I have no evidence of that. It was a pretty wise move on his behalf if he did, because it then gave him protection from the Genovese family, for being a snitch-rat-stool-pigeon on Anthony. I'm not aware if he is still alive or not. The other fact is that Jackie had two kids that I know of and a beautiful wife. Just another testimony to how hard it was to stay faithful to a wife because of beautiful women often coming on to us.

Anthony had been found guilty, even though he had supposedly bribed a New York Cardinal to testify at his trial what a good and faithful Catholic Christian he was. I was told that the bribe to the church was for $250,000. However, since I was not there when it was supposedly given, it is only a rumor. I do know that a cardinal was at the trial, he did testify in Anthony's favor, and Anthony was given a personalized painting of the last supper with a varathane finish on a wood plaque (much like Michael Corleone in the *Godfather 2*).

Union Delegate...
Loves to Fly

I was having some problems with my truck drivers in the trucking company that I was running which was a pickup and delivery air freight service (PU&D) trucking company for Emery Air Freight. I know I had explained this earlier but wanted to reiterate it for this issue. I handled all of Westchester and Orange County, NY and part of Fairfield county Connecticut. I had started off at this barn as a driver, after leaving as a driver for Breen Airfreight Trucking. There was a dispatcher who worked for the trucking company and a manager who was hired by Emery Air Freight as the terminal manager.

I drove or worked all of the routes over a few months getting a feel and understanding of the different routes, the stops, the shipping personnel and the customers and their intricacies including distances, traffic, time, etc. The trucking company was partly owned by Anthony and the plan was that I was to eventually run the company. So I needed to know the score on everything from the routes, to the drivers and their abilities. I could tell that no one was happy with me as a new driver because I wasn't someone from the union hall, which was the union's normal way of hiring. I put up with their snide remarks and attitude toward me because I eventually knew what the end result would be, and I'd have the last laugh. I worked hard and tried to make friends of the drivers, but most were unfriendly.

After a few months of this I was moved into the dispatcher's position and the company's existing union dispatcher was let go. I felt for him because he was a good guy, but I didn't make the decision and I needed the work, and a healthy raise. It was only after about 6 months that I personally had the Emery Air Freight manager himself

124

removed. As I pointed out and proved to Emery, he was dead weight, and served only as a watchdog. He had been with Emery for 20 years so I'm sure they found a place for him after we had him removed from what then became my barn.

The problem was that the trucking pickup and delivery service was contracted out to our company (Dion Delivery Service). Emery received the freight from companies and private persons to forward via airlines to different countries, states, cities and eventually companies or private parties also. And Emery had us deliver freight to companies and persons in the areas where we had control.

I tried to fit into the driver's good graces and some of them accepted me because I did a good job and wanted to treat them fairly. Since I had become the manager, I changed things as I thought necessary. That's what they didn't agree with since there was a shop steward and assistant shop steward who both seemed to hold me off from getting to know them. They definitely were pulling as much union crap as possible. I tried to really show the drivers that I wasn't against them but wanted to work as a good unit. The better we were as a team, the more work we would get, and the work force would increase. There were days when we worked into the late hours of night to get the enormous amount of freight sorted, packed and on the way to the airports. I would often buy pizza and beer, after a big freight or long day.

The assistant shop steward was a large strong man who was originally from the deep south, and I believe hated 'northers' like me. One day he grabbed me by the lapels of my sweater and started violently pushing me around. I automatically, punched him in the jaw. Not with a lot of power, only enough to let him know that more would be coming, if he didn't calm down. He realized what he was doing and how it could get him fired. It did. I fired him and told him to get off the dock and out of the building.

The shop steward asked me to have a quiet conversation with him concerning the incident. We went into my office and he explained to me that the assistant shop steward had a very sick son and he was very upset of recent news that he'd received that morning. Consequently, I had compassion on him and hired him back. IT

DIDN'T CHANGE ANYTHING! He and the shop steward were just as arrogant and uncooperative as they had been.

Emery had a total of three male salespersons that worked with me in our territory trying to increase production. The problem was that they were not very successful. One of them left for whatever reason and I requested that Emery have a woman replace him. There was a reason for this. I had some companies that I knew would increase our production considerably. But every time I sent one of the male salesmen to go to them, they would be kept waiting a long time and were not being allowed to meet with the company's management, seldom got even one piece of freight. When I sent the new cute woman into just those accounts, she would be introduced to the shipping personnel and the management and was never kept waiting. And she sold our Dion Delivery Service and Emery's services to companies that had not yet been using us. I then requested for all the salespersons to be women. But it was 1970 and later and that didn't happen, even though they would have been better. Now women, start the wheels turning. Yes, she was cute, and more important, very smart. She sold more accounts in six months than three men did in three years. Partially because she was able to get the larger companies when the men were not. Also, as I said, not only was she pretty, but really smart and knew how to talk to people, getting their attention and respect.

In the five years that I was there, I quadrupled Emery's forwarding in our area. But all was not wonderful or easy in any way. I hired new drivers as the production increased and treated the drivers with respect for their good work. I listened to their requests and especially their suggestions. But the union was working against me the whole way.

One instance occurred when my dispatcher started having trouble at least once a week (for weeks) trying to contact any of our drivers on their truck radios, when they left the barn going toward their routes in the morning. This was unusual and illogical. I decided to follow the last truck when it left the barn one day and found that it stopped at a diner only a few miles down the road. To my amazement all of the trucks were there. After I watched the last driver walk into the diner, I also went in. All the men were down at one end of the diner eating and having coffee while this union delegate was preaching to them, standing up like some kind of a preacher. I sat down at the counter on the far side having coffee and listened to this mutt spill his crap. He was telling my drivers that they were working too hard, doing too many stops per day, and should slow down so that we would have to hire additional drivers. There was some conversation on how to do that, and then he said that he was trying to have me removed so that they could put in a union person to manage the barn.

That's when I stood up and walked over to where they were all sitting. When they saw me there was a look of fear on their faces because they knew I could fire them all. That's when this delegate turned around, and after recognizing me, said that I should go because he was having a union meeting with his members. He stressed that I wasn't invited. I told him to take his cup of coffee and shove it up his fat ass. Then I told the men that since they were on my time clock, and they were not working but had met there without permission, I would fire every one of them and make this terminal a nonunion one, while everything got settled, which could be a long, long time. I also said that all they had to do was ask this fat mutt of a delegate what happened down at Breen Air Freight when they were on strike. They looked at the delegate and since he had little to say, because he knew not only was he in the wrong, but that I'd bust his fat ass, they left. This delegate and I walked outside together and had a few words before we left. I wanted to send him to the hospital but decided that I didn't need the trouble that I would be left with.

It was a few days later when I was informed that the head of union local 295 and his delegate were going to meet with me and my boss/associate, at my terminal in two days. I was looking forward to it with all my heart. I hated both these men, primarily because I always hated unions. They thought they had a lot more clout than they did concerning me.

The day came and the four of us met in my office at the terminal. We had some heated discussion on both sides and then I invited the delegate to go out on the dock and have a private discussion to try to come to an agreement together. My associate knew me, so he said that it wasn't necessary. But the union boss agreed that we should have some time to settle our differences in private. The only problem was that I hated both of these mutts, so I didn't play fair, and that's what my associate and boss knew from the beginning. He knew that I was good at running trucking but lousy with guys like this.

When we were on the dock our associates were talking and occasionally watching us through the windows. We started off just discussing what we had been talking about inside. Then I told him that if he met with my men again without my knowing it, I'd give him a beating that he'd never forget. I said all of this with a smile on my face, so that while we were being watched I looked like it was being friendly. He turned to me and asked me to say it again. I said, "You probably didn't hear what I said, because of the shit in your ears from having your head up your boss's ass," again with a smile. Then he let out a scream and took a swing at me.

Now he was as tall as me and at least forty pounds heavier. But I was in much better shape. I pared his punch off with a forearm. Then began my job of beating his fat ass all over the dock. It happened so fast that our associates didn't know what to do. Before they came out of the office and started toward us, yelling at us to of course stop fighting. I had this mutt out on the dock slab. I grabbed him by the back of the suit jacket, and the back of his pants belt, picked him up, despite his large girth, and swung him onto his car's front windshield, which was parked front end first up to the dock. He crashed partially through the windshield and landed on his hood, steering wheel and dashboard and he didn't look too comfortable. I may have gone a little too far! Nah! Screw him and his boss.

I felt good! However, my boss/associate was not too happy, and neither was the union boss. They were yelling and asking what the hell happened to cause this. I told them that I was trying to just talk to him and explain my side as we did inside. I said that the meeting in the diner without asking me, was inappropriate and that's when he started to yell and insult me. Finally, he said that I was an asshole. That's when he doubled up his fists and took a swing at me. You must have seen that he took the first swing, right? Then I said,

"Obviously, it was the wrong move. So then I only thought that he wanted to go home, so I showed him to his car." All the while this union leader was nearly blowing his top wanting to kill me. This is why he later put a contract out on my life.

About a month later. I was supposed to have a meeting with the head of Teamsters Local. He was present when I threw his big, scumbag delegate through his windshield. I was told that he wanted to meet away from everybody and cool the air. When the arrangements were made to meet in a bar in Queens, I thought that there was a reason that was not in my favor. The years of street knowledge made me very cautious of this "supposed" meeting. Well, I did have a meeting but not what they had suggested.

I went to the place of the proposed meeting later in the day after work, and when I walked in, the bar was empty with only the bartender standing behind the bar. Already, I was very cautious and thinking that this was a setup. The bar being empty was not the real issue. Many times, when we were having a meeting that we didn't want outsiders around us, we were sure to have the premises empty. It cost money, but it helped to keep it clear because in case a bystander decided to rat on what he may have heard. So...clear the place out!

I was walking in very cautiously thinking that I would be having a drink at the bar, knowing that the entire bar was empty including the bartender. Because as soon as he saw me, he had gone inside the kitchen. As I was starting to walk in, I saw a shadow of a guy moving swiftly into the light from around a corner of a back room, and at the same time raising his arm that had a pistol in it.

As I said I was already cautious when this all happened, so I immediately started to move and dive for the floor while I was grabbing for my gun behind my back. I heard a shot while I was in the air and returned fire, once while in the air and once I was on the ground, and I fired two more while trying to see him through the table and chair legs. At the same time, he came around by the far end of the bar and took another shot where he thought that I had landed. Neither of us hit one another, and he left just as quick as he came. Apparently, he didn't like being shot at, and only liked shooting at someone by complete surprise. Chicken shit hit man!

When I thought it was reasonably safe, I cautiously got up off the floor while keeping an eye at the area where he had entered and escaped. I cautiously went to the bar where the bartender had reappeared. He probably thought that I was dead and needed to see that so he could then call the cops. I kept my gun on the door while I grabbed the bartender by the collar and dragged him across the bar. He fell onto the floor face first, and I dragged him up in front of me. He had gone away from the bar because he knew what was going to happen. If this hit man came in shooting again, it would be him that took the hits, not me. He tried to run away, when I hit him in the head with my gun hard enough to make him understand that I would go further if it became necessary. He held onto his bleeding head while I pushed him out of the restaurant in front of me, holding him as a human shield. I took him all the way to the car, very slowly and very cautiously. Just before I got in my car, I punched this scumbag in the face several times. Breaking is nose and God knows that else, because he was on the ground moaning like the Mutt that he was. I told him that I knew that he knew that I was to be killed in his bar. I also explained exactly who I was and who I was associated with, because if there were any repercussions, he would suffer immensely for helping to set me up. I stood there waiting for some kind of another attack on me, but it didn't happen. I waited because I didn't want to bring it home with me. After a while, I went directly home that evening. I drove the next day to Lewisburg to see Anthony as soon as I could.

In the morning, when the prison was allowing visitors. I was one of the first to be let in. Guys like Anthony weren't held to the same standards as the rest of the inmates. I was allowed to see him when I asked. When he came into the visiting area, he saw the look on my face, and knew that something was up. Now he was a great actor, so I couldn't read his face as to whether he knew about the hit or not. He asked me what the matter was, and I asked him if he was the one who put a hit on me. He jumped out of his chair and the guards nearly jumped on him. Then he sat down and asked if I really believed that he could have me killed. I told him yes without a doubt in my mind. The question was, "Did you?" He cracked up, and said, "I've said this before and I'll say it again, you never ever stop surprising me."

Then he said, "No I didn't put a hit on you, so tell me what happened. You have to believe me. You know that if I did, I would also tell you that it was me and I'd tell you why." This was true because there would be no place to hide.

I told him of the incidence, and he said that I was very lucky to have been alive. He also asked what in the world was I doing out of our area where we know the clubs, the restaurants, the streets, the bars, the bartenders, hell even the streetlights. I told him that I thought that maybe I could settle this strike, since I had pretty much caused it. He smiled and said to go home and get some sleep. And not to worry about any more attempts on my life, because before I was back in New Jersey, the whole issue would be taken care of, including the guy who attempted the hit. I told him that I didn't want anyone killed. He said then why were you carrying a gun and why did you return fire. I explained that I have it to protect myself, if needed. It wasn't to kill anyone, unless I had to. He said the problem was that if the guy was a professional, he still had an obligation to fulfill the contract. But not to worry, it would all be taken care of. Maybe this guy will want to, or already has, decided to leave the country since I was not only one of Anthony's men but his son-in-law. We talked a while and then I left for New Jersey to change and go back to my office in Westchester County in the afternoon, since my dispatcher was now the one running the barn.

So now I was totally pissed, and the union boss had to know it. He also knew that if something happened to me, worse would happen to him. I received a phone call from the union headquarters requesting a meeting the following day with Harry in his office. I figured that a meeting in his office would be not only safe but a good time to straighten out our differences. The primary differences were having the men at a secret meeting when they are on the clock. Also, that they shouldn't be told to slow down so that more men are necessary because it obviously cuts into the profits, and he knew who got part of that.

The next morning, I went to the Teamster's office and told the receptionist who I was, and that I had an appointment with Harry. She told me that she would let Harry know that I was there. I sat down and started reading some magazines while I waited. I reminded the receptionist that I was still waiting and then realized that I had been there for about an hour total. I again went to the receptionist and was told that Harry was too busy today, and I should call for another appointment. I explained that it was Harry who called me for an appointment today, not me. She then said that he said he was too busy to see me.

I realized that he had planned for me to wait, and not have the meeting from the get-go. I also knew that it was him that set me up to be shot in the bar, because I was there to meet with him. I was furious! I'm six feet, five inches and a door is typically six-foot-eight. The top hinge is just about level with my shoulder. And since I have been studying and practicing karate for a few years now, where I have learned how to break boards and bricks, I used flat or palm of my hand right at the area of the top hinge with all my might and the door fell into the hallway. I had to step on the door breaking the bottom hinge and partially flattening the door on the floor and up onto the opposite wall, while I stepped into the hallway. At that time a couple of drivers who were in the lounge area came into the hallway to see what all the commotion was. The crash of the door and the scream of the receptionist made them come running. I was now walking toward them, and they just retreated to the kitchen area where they had come from. Harry's office was at the end to the hallway. I opened the door and went through as I saw Harry looking at me with absolute surprise and hatred in his eyes. He then pulled his top drawer out, trying to grab his revolver. But I was already running toward the desk as soon as I saw him opening the drawer. It was a short distance and I made it to the desk in time to slam the drawer closed on his hand. He hadn't yet grabbed the gun and I let his hand out of the drawer and took the gun out. I emptied the cartridges onto the floor while yelling and explaining why I had done what I did. It was beyond acceptable to request me to come to his office (out near Kennedy airport) and keep me waiting for an hour, and then not see me on purpose. I knew that he was just doing it to aggravate me, and it worked. I also told him that I knew it was him that put a hit on me, and reminded him that not only did I get my way through it, but I believe that it was permanently taken care of, because I went to Lewisburg and saw Anthony. I could see in his face that he knew he was not only wrong but had screwed with the wrong people. I then left and went to my office back in Rye, New York.

Nothing came of it, other than the men who were picketing my barn started to become mouthier. I remembered when I broke the union picket line at Breen in NYC. That they were apparently told to shoot at my truck and shot out my windshield and my tire. They weren't trying to kill me, only teach me a lesson. After all of this, I was given two men to act as bodyguards. Believe it or not they were Vinnie and Louie. They were about ten or twelve inches shorter than me and definitely seventy to eighty pounds lighter, but every pound, tough as nails.

I came out of my office one afternoon and a bunch of my drivers were holding weapons like two-by-fours and bats, in an attempt to scare me, I guess. Vinnie and Louie were behind me and when they came out and walked down the stairs to the parking lot with me, they stood alongside me. It was three against probably twelve men. Vinnie looked at the shop steward who was the tallest and biggest of the group and said, as he was pointing toward him, "He's mine."

Then Louie points at the next to the biggest driver and says, "He's mine."

Now the drivers are holding their proposed weapons and there's a lot more of them. Their most likely thinking *yeah, I'll bust you up.* But then Vinnie, Louie, and I open our suit jackets and showed the drivers that we had guns tucked in our waistbands. We were ready to roll with them and see what happened. I knew how tough these two were and what my capabilities were. We didn't take hold of them, or pull them out, just showed them in their waistbands, so that they would drop their weapons. When the drivers saw that, they literally ran to their vehicles. Started them up and backed out like a bunch of comical Keystone Cops.

That union strike ended thanks to Anthony while he was still incarcerated in Lewisburg. All went back as it was with exception of me and the dispatcher really keeping track of where they were. Life went on, and caution was always part of it!

Anthony's Escape
and My Death

I received a call while in my office and was asked to meet that evening with The Brush and Moon at a Steak House in downtown NYC. This steak house was, and maybe still is the best in NYC. I had no idea why, but in fact the request was finalized with "as soon as possible." After setting up my night manager and believing that all would be okay at the trucking terminal, I left for the restaurant about an hour after the call.

It took the usual hour to get down to the restaurant and "Moon" and "The Brush" were at the bar waiting for me. When I arrived, we went directly into the back room where we often met for complete privacy. Moon started off the conversation by telling me that he had the restaurant, especially this room, swept just this afternoon to be sure we had complete privacy and we could talk freely. It was common for us to be concerned about being taped or overheard.

The mood in the room was thick, and I wondered if I was going to walk out of there alive. I had no idea what this was about. I positioned myself in a manner that gave me as much room as possible, so I could react to any life-threatening situation that might arise suddenly. I was always aware that The Brush never liked me. I was in a position to defend myself as quickly as possible. As we were talking, I walked backward as to place the conference table between us. As it was, it wasn't really about me, but about my help, instead.

Let me digress a little and lay out some information that is necessary before I get to the meeting and what it was about. As mentioned earlier Anthony had been incarcerated in Lewisburg Prison, and then transferred to a minimum-security prison farm, in Allenwood, in

Pennsylvania, about two hundred miles from my home. I had been visiting him and because we were talking in prison, things that were discussed concerning much of our dealings, were done with absolute privacy. As to what was about to be discussed and later take place could only be brought up at our favorite restaurant where it was safe to talk.

It was July 1972 and Anthony had already been incarcerated for a year and was also under an additional two federal indictments. Anthony was now locked up in Federal House of Detention in NYC. He had also learned that he was now under indictment for a "labor racketeering" charge filed by Brooklyn Strike Force Against Organized Crime.

He had convinced the warden, Louis Gengler, in Lewisburg to allow him to be incarcerated in NYC so that he could have his dental caps completed by the same dentist who had started the work on his teeth, whom he'd already paid generously for the entire procedure. He had threatened a lawsuit, if you can believe it, if the work was not completed by his personal and prepaid dentist. Remember, he was not put in prison for a violent crime or anything like that; he was in there for what is considered "white-collar crime."

In the event you don't know what a white-collar crime is, it's a crime such as stealing or fraud. In general, it is not a violent crime. His crimes were the theft of a million in negotiable bonds, and having the bonds sent over state lines to be sold, which made it a federal crime.

Well, they consented by sending him to NYC to get the work on his teeth completed with the original dentist on Long Island. The Lewisburg prison warden told the New York Times that allowing prisoners out with good records was an accepted practice with the Federal System of incarceration. However, the warden stated that he only learned about the new indictments by the state of New York after Anthony had already gone to the dentist for the third time. He was going to cancel Anthony's allowance to be out of prison control when Anthony returned to the NYC jail that day.

The arrangement was that two FBI agents would accompany him to the dentist, wait for the work to be done each day and then return him to the West Street Jail. As this program continued for three days, Anthony was able to "convince" (I was told, bribing with large amounts of cash) the agents to allow him to go to one of our trucking companies (located in Long Island) on the way back to NYC, so he could visit "friends." On the third day they allowed him to stay there eventually "by himself" and return to the prison in NYC, on his own. However, he did not!

Getting back to the restaurant and our conversation, our discussion was to arrange my involvement in his escape during his dental appointment outing. The plans were discussed and agreed to that night. His brother (Moon) was to pick him up right after he arrived at the Long Island trucking company and deliver him to meet me in Stanford Connecticut. I was to aid Anthony's escape by driving him into Canada. I was the most reasonable "volunteer" for this job, since I had no convictions and was just a trucking manager who was associated to the Genovese family through Anthony, but not a "made" member. Also, the rest of Anthony's associates, including his brother, would be running the feds and police all over the city in complete confusion, as they searched for Anthony there.

Here's the hard part of the deal: as always (and in everything we did) no one was to know, including my wife. The thing to remember is if a person is privy to actions that are illegal, and they are questioned concerning an illegal action by let's say the FBI. And if they admit that they knew of the actions in question, they could be held or arrested as being a part of the crime. If they didn't admit that they knew, and the FBI found out that they did, then they could be charged and arrested for interfering with an investigation by withholding the information. Bottom line is actions like what was going to happen, and others could never be shared with anyone, especially your wife, family, or friends. I believe that I told her I was going on a trip with some associates to Florida for a conference and short work vacation with my trucking associates.

Anthony was brought out to meet me in his 1971 powder blue Mercedes 450SL convertible, which we drove directly up to Toronto, Canada. His brother drove him to me and was picked up by someone else to return to NYC. The drive to Canada was about 350 miles which took about seven hours. We had to keep to the speed limit, of course, and went over the border around three in the afternoon. We drove up in his Mercedes because it was now left to his wife while he was in prison, and we knew the FBI would be going out of their minds looking for him. They wouldn't consider his wife in any way, since she was as innocent as a dove. All the wives were never told anything that could get them in trouble with the law or say something to anyone that would get us in trouble either. Of course, we and the Mercedes would be in Canada before they even began looking for him. I would have preferred parking it in some undisclosed place in NY, New Jersey, or even CT, instead of having to drive it with him as my passenger. Then returning to the states with it. But I wasn't the mastermind, only the requested driver. The idea was that if I used my car and went through the Canadian Border Control and the license was tabulated, I would definitely be arrested for helping a convict to escape. If his plates were somehow observed, it could have been anyone driving it, including Anthony.

The question as to why did he need a driver was that not only did he not have a driver's license since he had been incarcerated, and if he were stopped for any reason, his face would be seen while dealing with the policeman or State Trooper. Being a passenger, rather than a driver, would keep him from being focused on. (By the way, never, I say NEVER, mess with a New York State Trooper.)

WHY would we be in his distinctive Mercedes convertible (with the top down) driving toward the Canadian border in broad daylight? This was because Anthony wanted to feel as free as he could in case we got pinched on the way up. I, on the other hand was not so excited about driving with the top down since I would be joining him in prison if we were pinched. Anthony said no one would recognize us, because they wouldn't be looking for us yet. As we were passing through the Canadian checkpoint (me with an escaped convict) he even spoke kindly to the officer telling him to have a nice day. After getting through the checkpoint (having fake IDs for any occasion needed) I asked him why he was letting the officer see his face. He told me that looking directly at the guy would be less suspicious than looking away, since border guards are trained to look for anything unusual. That information helped me later, when I used to bring him hundreds of thousands of dollars taped to my body going through South American, Brazilian customs. But that's another story! So we drove right through without any problem. To an apartment that was already rented, furnished, with fake IDs for him and me, and ready for his occupancy in Toronto, Canada.

There is so much more to this than can even be explained. For example, I was often being tailed either by car or by helicopter from when I left my house until I got to work. My phone was tapped at home and work for years. Therefore, extra clothing couldn't just be packed in a suitcase and carried to my car, even with my car parked in the garage. If my wife saw it, she would then be aware of some knowledge which could put her in a position of criminal liability and might even say something to me or someone else that could be overheard. I didn't even let my wife know that I was taking clothing in my valise. Everything had to go very quietly (like clockwork) from his exchange into a car at the trucking terminal in Long Island, to the next exchange into his car, my meeting with him in Stanford, the drive up to Canada, crossing the border, and finding the apartment with no tails, stops, tickets or being pinched. I'm getting nervous just retelling it.

I was there with him when he was now "on the Lam" (hiding from the law) when we were notified that the Feds were told to shoot on sight. Clearly the bribed federal agents (and I was told the Warden), would have liked this incident to be closed as soon as possible without too many questions. All I knew was what he confided in me while I was with him in Canada. And dead men don't talk!

When I would return to see him, several times, he had fake ID's, he let his hair and beard grow over time and, of course, wore clothing and hats that gave some additional cover. When I was there, we were up in the AM very early, and he went jogging in a nearby park, under cover of early morning darkness. I say he because I didn't last long, but he was in great shape from his exercising while in prison. I was no doubt very strong, but putting on weight due to lack of exercise, eating too much, and drinking every day. We jogged and then went back to the apartment to shower, eat, and spend the rest of the day either reading, talking or just thinking. His apartment had a room that was furnished as a library with a beautiful view of the park.

That's where we had most of our conversations with soft low music in the background, sitting on leather easy chairs looking at the view. And that's where Anthony told me about how he had ordered that I be killed the night he had called me downtown to Ponte's restaurant to meet with him, when I had told him that his daughter was pregnant. I should mention or remind the reader that the restaurant was owned by "made" men. I know that one of the brothers (possibly all three) were "made men." "Made men" are those who are accepted into any crime family as soldiers or above. In this case, I'm referring to the Genovese Family, and a requirement of acceptance into any family is that you are of 100 percent Italian heritage. I couldn't ever have been "made," thank you, God!

He then told me that after I had told him that his daughter and I had eloped, instead of waiting to have the huge wedding that he was planning for her. He had already known that we were going to be married (even though he couldn't stand the sight of me) and he had already started to make arrangements with the Americana hotel in NYC for the reception. He was finally going to see his daughter receive an abundance of monetary "gifts" from his associates. His generosity to other brides and grooms had, over the years, been frequent and apparent at the weddings of the sons and daughters of others. This kind of event would have promised us a great amount of money. I was told the probability at least $70,000. He asked me when my wife and I were sitting with him at the restaurant, and why we had gotten married so soon. I had to be the one to tell him, her father, and now my well-known mafia father-in-law that she was pregnant. He wanted to kill me right then, but my wife, his daughter was with me. So after some very nervous conversation and shaking of his legs under the table in the restaurant, we were told to go home. Eloping meant that we were now married with a child on its way, and broke.

Now remember that I was having this conversation with him while in his Toronto, Canada apartment. No one knew where I was, with exception of his closest associates.

He began by reminding me that he had called me and requested me to meet with him back at the restaurant the night after I had told him that his daughter was pregnant. This was requested to a guy he already didn't like (maybe it would be closer to and was, hated). When I arrived at the restaurant that next night, I went upstairs to the bar where Anthony, and his associates Jackie the Nose and Philly The Brush were standing, he asked if I wanted a drink. There was a guy I learned that was to make sure no one entered into the bar from the restaurant until he was told it was okay. I got a shot of Scotch on the rocks. At that time is when the plan was to go into action.

He told me that his two associates were told to push me into the kitchen, through the door which was located at the same end of the bar where we already were standing. He asked if I remember that when I walked in, the bartender went directly onto the kitchen. I told him I did. Then he told me that when he went into the kitchen, all the help was told that it was "break time" for all of them to clear out the kitchen. So they were now all downstairs and outside, and also told to stay outside until they were told to come back in. They had no idea what was about to happen and also had not seen me in the bar. I was then to be shoved into the kitchen, where they were to open my gut with a butcher's knife, already placed on a counter. Additionally, the bartender and owner, after making sure that everyone was gone, had already placed a plastic sheet where I was to be opened like a clam. The bartender then returned to the bar to serve me my drink. The drink was to show me some friendliness before I was to be killed. Then I was to be put in the dumbwaiter that goes down into the garage, where they would put me in a car trunk that had also already been lined with plastic sheeting. Lastly, they would dump my "worthless ass" into the East River with a heavy weight attached to my feet never to be seen again. Now there's a conversation to have when no one knows where you are, and you're alone with an escaped Mafia underboss!

I was at the end of the bar sipping on some scotch, waiting to see why I had been requested to meet him there. I knew that he hated me, but had to show up or be labeled scared, which was not an option for me. Not even my new bride knew that I had gone there to meet him, because he told me to not tell anyone including her. But while we were still having a sip of our scotch at the end of the bar. I remembered seeing the guy, who was guarding the bar entrance, stick his head inside quickly while I sat sipping scotch. Then, very shortly, two men walked in and spoke to the owner, and bartender, Joey. It turned out that these two men were FBI agents who promptly asked if Anthony was there. Apparently, they were able to make it past the doorman by showing him their badges. Luckily, just before the feds entered the bar, the doorman was able to alert Joey who immediately notified Anthony and his "associates" (the would-be assassins) that the Feds were at the other end of the bar. I was then immediately told to "beat it." My fate changed because the FBI agents walked in. Little did THEY know their mere appearance saved my life and ultimately opened the door for me to assist Anthony in his escape from Federal imprisonment years later. I now believe that my life being spared was due to God's plan and involvement, not Anthony's or the FBIs.

That evening, after being told about the plan to murder me in '67, I was to sleep in his apartment in Canada. I couldn't help worrying that perhaps a new plan to off me had been established. Even though by this time I believed he respected, and, I thought, loved me like a son, because of how I handled myself with work, requests, and helping him escape. However, I also knew that you never knew when you would be wacked (killed) even by a friend or relative. The first time I slept there after hearing that story, I tossed and turned. Hopefully he didn't feel he had to dispose of me as a form of insurance that his current whereabouts would not be exposed.

After what felt like a safe time, I prepared to head back to New York. To play it safe, I avoided crossing the border at the same point by traveling further west in Canada until I could go through Detroit, Michigan and then head east to NYC. Before going home to New Jersey, I met with some associates who knew and appreciated what I had done for Anthony. We wanted to have a drink together in celebration of Anthony's freedom. When I got to the restaurant, my car had been brought there and I left Anthony's Mercedes with "Moon."

I wasn't in NYC more than an hour when I was arrested by the FBI. They used the same scare tactics, with a few smacks and it wasn't any more than another hour or so before I was released with no charges for a few reasons. First, that's what a good, crooked lawyer, money, and a plan devised before I left could do. All I knew was that they got no information from me and the attorney had been on stand-by, ready to come and get me released even before I had been arrested. Also, the FBI had no reason to arrest me, because they had no idea if anyone assisted Anthony in his escape. There was no proof. They likely zeroed in on me because I rode into NYC in Anthony's Mercedes and I had been missing for a few days. Of course, they wanted to know where I had been. My response was, "With your wife." Not good!

As I had mentioned, I went to see him with messages and questions and returned to NYC with his answers and demands. I was there a few times. I was always met at the Montreal airport by a young woman who then drove me to a restaurant. After dining, we headed to her condo which was in the same building as Anthony's apartment. That way the FBI would believe that I went to Canada to be with her, if they were in some way following me.

Anthony had a favorite place near his apartment in Montreal that he liked to eat called "The Old Mill." It was a beautiful old mill that at one time was turned into a church, then into a five-star restaurant, inn, bar, hotel, and conference center. They had an orchestra and a large dance floor off the dining room, which was and is still very memorable.

In fact, I even brought my wife to see her father once. I was against that, but who the hell was I to offer an opinion? I was just a pawn on the board of bishops, knights, queens, and kings that made the decisions, and I faithfully carried them out.

However, FBI problems did occur with the apartment that he was in, in the not too distant future.

Anthony was still on the "lam" in his apartment in Toronto Canada. When two of his girlfriends knocked on the door and explained that they had just been shown his photograph by FBI agents down in the lobby, asking if they knew or had seen him. They had told the agents no and then went directly to him. He thanked them for their discretion and told them to get away as fast as possible. They didn't live there so they had no problem doing just that.

He knew that he didn't have much time, so he threw some clothing into a paper bag and rushed down the many flights of stairs to escape to a bus a few blocks away to get him to the airport. He made the airport with no interruptions and got on a flight to Paris, France. From France, he flew to Germany, then to Greece, then to somewhere in Africa. Finally, he headed to Paraguay where he claimed political asylum.

I remember him telling me, while laughing, that he was really glad that he had several identifications that matched passports. He said it would have been a real red flag if he'd skipped from country to country with the same identity. One of the customs police would have definitely challenged him and the feds would have definitely caught up with him before he made it to Paraguay.

The Fed's found someone in Canada who identified Anthony as a resident of the building they suspected. So they entered the apartment and took fingerprints to see who had been there. Guess who came up? There I was again, arrested and questioned knowing that I had been there due to my fingerprints all over the place. Their only problem was that the attorney who again showed up within an hour, asked if they had a warrant to enter the premises. They did not. They were within the law to enter the apartment because they had information that that was where Anthony lived. But the attorney somehow found a flaw where the fingerprints apparently needed a warrant. I didn't even stay overnight in the slammer. I also have no idea how the attorney got me off. There may have been some bribe which was often the custom in those days.

It was about a year later when I was again requested to meet with Moon and The Brush again, privately, in the rear room. This time I was asked to consider bringing money to Anthony down in South America. And believe me it wasn't an easy decision! Moon had already been there and brought him money. But Moon was being watched very closely those days since they knew that Anthony was in South America.

They had a fake ID and passport for me and set up flights for two different trips over two years. The first one I flew out of Pennsylvania to Miami Florida, then to Brazil to meet with Anthony. He didn't want me to fly to Paraguay for some reason which I never found out. I got the feeling that both times we met in Brazil; he had some other business there to attend to as well. He met me in Rio de Janeiro both times. He had to meet me himself, even with the danger of being caught, because I had two hundred thousand dollars taped to my waist and legs to move through Brazilian customs. He didn't want to trust anyone down there to pick it up for him, for some reason. Imagine that!

I didn't stay there more than a few hours in both trips before I returned to the states and home. I believe that I will always remember the feeling of going through customs with hundreds of thousands of dollars taped to my body. I couldn't show any fear or concern in any way, especially being a six-foot-five and around 250 pounds, white boy coming from America. What Anthony had told me when we went over the Canadian border about the importance of being friendly, instead of watchful and nervous, was exactly how I got through.

When Anthony was in Paraguay, he married a Paraguayan woman and along with his political asylum, this really banded his ability to stay there. He even was in the process of purchasing a shipping company, which, apparently, was why he needed the cash.

All went well, until it didn't.

A couple of years after that, the FBI hired a local Paraguayan mafia-type group to kidnap him and bring him to Panama, where he was turned over to the FBI. Apparently, all is fair in love and war! From there he was brought to Florida and put in a federal prison there, while being interrogated as to who helped him escape. They thought it was me but couldn't use the fingerprint evidence because of it being illegally obtained. And they wanted him to give me up. They had an interesting method of doing that while he was there.

During the time he was in Florida jail, he wasn't allowed to make any phone calls or contact anyone. So no one knew where he was or what happened. In fact, his associates were concerned that he possibly had been killed down in Paraguay. He slept on the concrete floor with no covers or clothing and was woken up each morning by being kicked, sometimes in the head or teeth. He said that they kept him up until the early morning hours so that he would be so tired he might slip and let out some information during hours of intense questioning. Also, because he was so tired, he had to be woken up by them, not on his own. After a while they knew that he wouldn't rat on me or any of us who had a hand in his escape so they brought him up to New York again. Once there, he was tried again and sent up to a federal prison in the Federal Correctional Institute in Lake Placid, New York.

I visited him only twice while he was up there because my wife had taken my children to Santa Fe, NM after our separation. And I was out of my mind wanting to be with my kids, so a year after she left, I also moved south and wound up in San Diego, CA, which was much closer to Santa Fe, than NYC. I couldn't stay in Santa Fe where the children were, because, rightfully, my wife didn't want me there. So I chose San Diego.

Why Not be NICE?

Getting back to my life in New York: I had a driver named Sal in one of the air freight trucking companies that I managed who was one of my best drivers. He was above and beyond all the other drivers that I had in my trucking company. Although he was a union worker, he believed in doing his work with as much concern and honesty as possible. I used to occasionally tell him that he should stay at home for the day and he would still get paid. In fact, there were days when we used to go and play golf together because I gave him the day off, paid.

He was very responsible and also a handsome and a very tough Italian man who was small in stature. He was small in stature but definitely not in ability. I often used him as an example to kids or young men who would say to me that they wish that they were my size. I would then and still do tell them a wise saying. "It's not the size of the dog in the fight, it's the size of the fight in the dog." Then I tell them about this situation I was confronted with concerning this driver, and friend, Sal.

He was on an early "special delivery" of air freight to a company in downtown New York City. He turned onto a street to get to his delivery destination that had to be there every day by seven in the morning. There was a garbage truck in the middle of the one-way road that blocked him from going any further.

He got out of the truck and walked up to this really big man (I know because I met him) who was grabbing cans of garbage off the sidewalk and putting it into the rear of the garbage truck. He nicely explained that he needed to get around the garbage truck to make an important delivery, and asked him if he would have the driver pull into an available, empty parking space not too far ahead. (I wasn't there, but I know this man and he is always nice until he is pushed too far.) The guy agreed and walked up to converse with the driver before returning to the rear again and continuing with his work.

The truck moved up to where the empty spot was and didn't pull in to let my driver past as he had requested. Sal got out and asked the guy why they didn't pull into the spot as requested so he could get by. The man answered, "Tough shit, ya little guinea prick. We'll move when we want and where we want, so get the hell out of my face, you little punk."

Being called a "little guinea prick" really set Sal off! He jumped in the air and hit this guy in the face and continued to beat the snot out of him.

I should tell you something about Sal's method of fighting. One day, I saw Sal jump in the air to hit a guy who was at least a foot or more taller and about a hundred pounds heavier than him, on the dock. That guy had also made a mistake of insulting Sal's size. When Sal hit the guy, he had jumped in the air so that his full roundhouse swing was supported by his entire body weight right through his shoulder, continuing into his arm, and through his fist. Sal apparently had developed that style ever since he was a kid because of his small build. Although small, he was tough as nails and strong enough, because the guy went down like a sack of potatoes. I saw this whole thing from my office window. I also saw that after this guy could get off the ground, he smiled at Sal and apparently apologized. Then they shook hands and, in fact, became friends. Sal had proven his real height to him.

So Sal, keeping with his technique, hit this garbage man the same way. Unfortunately for this rude garbage man, he happened to be in an unfortunate location. Sal was able to throw him into the back of the truck while pulling the lever that moved the compacting panel shoving this guy deeper into the trash collection. As you can imagine, the guy is screaming by this point to the garbage truck driver who jumped out and ran to the rear of the truck to try and help his co-worker.

The driver is also bigger than Sal and he takes a swing at him. Sal ducked the punch and managed to deck him and throw him into the back of the trash truck along with his friend. Both garbage men were cursing loudly by this point and people were taking notice. Soon, a policeman came running around the corner and saw Sal holding them in and trying to compact them into the truck along with the trash. He stopped Sal and arrested him on the spot holding him in jail for attempted manslaughter.

I got a phone call from Sal while he was in the police station. He explained what happened and asked if I could help him out. After I hung up with Sal it took a while until I could stop laughing. I went down to the police station after making a call to a man that I knew very well who owned the garbage business. I explained that the garbage man called Sal a little guinea. The owner of the garbage business is also an Italian and agreed to go to the police station and confront his men. I had asked him to order his men to drop the charges and tell the police that it was a mistake because they were all just messing around, due to a bet they had made. He also told them that they are fired because of their actions and name-calling of an Italian brother.

He not only owned the garbage business, but was also a "made man," and everybody knew that, especially the police. So both the men asked for the charges to be dropped, or they would pay the consequences. Sal was released, and I brought him to the impound lot and got his truck out. "Fight in the dog, not the size of the dog in the fight."

Helping Out a Good Man

I had another incident with a driver named Ben, who was of African American descent. He was also a good, honest man and a hard worker who I appreciated and liked.

Ben was in a Harlem bar one evening where he lived, when he became so drunk that he passed out laying his head on the table where he was seated. Another black guy playing pool sees that Ben is passed out and picks his pockets. He takes Ben's money out of his wallet, throws the wallet on the table and goes back to playing pool as if nothing happened.

When Ben comes to his senses, he sees his wallet on the table and finds out that his money had been stolen from it, and his pockets had been picked of loose bills also. One of the men at the bar, who is a friend of Ben's, quietly pulls him aside and tells him what had happened and points out the guy was who stole his money.

Ben goes up to the guy (who is much larger than Ben) and confronts him, demanding that he return his money. The thief shoves Ben back onto a pool table and hit him when he comes back off the table, knocking him to the floor.

Ben realized that he is not going to be able to fight this guy, because he is so much bigger, and Ben is not a fighter. He leaves the bar and goes out to his car. He gets his pistol out of his trunk and heads back inside. He points the gun at the thief and, again, demands his money back. The thief doesn't believe that Ben will shoot him, so he comes at Ben with the intent to hit him again. Ben had pulled the hammer back on the pistol to get the thief to take him seriously. The thief then walked up to Ben and he pushed him hard! That push made Ben accidently pull the trigger and the thief is shot in the gut. He goes down, the police and ambulance are called, and

Ben is arrested for attempted murder. Luckily, the guy lives when he is taken to the hospital.

The next day, Ben called me from jail, because he had no one else to call to help him. He had a family and was a hard worker but didn't have anyone to help him in a situation like this. Few Do! He explained what happened and I told him I would do what I could to help him.

I immediately called a friend of mine who is also associated to Anthony over the years and asked him for a favor. I explain the situation and ask him if he can make a call to a guy, we both know, and ask him to help. I know that the guy I'm thinking of has a good attorney on retainer. The attorney was not on retainer for Ben or me, but he was asked to go and see what he could do as a favor to the "made" guy that was asking for me. No one owed me anything, especially him. But because I was a standup guy who was related to Anthony "Hickey" and doing a great job with the trucking companies, the attorney agrees and goes to the jail and talks with Ben.

It took a few days before Ben was brought before a judge, and the attorney was there to help. The entire situation at the bar and the shooting was explained to the judge, along with the fact that the mutt that was shot wasn't hurt very badly. It was still considered attempted murder, and Ben didn't have a permit for the pistol, but he had compassion for Ben, especially since he had absolutely no prior problems with the law. The mutt who stole Ben's money and hit him, had a bunch of priors, which also aided in the judge's decision. His decision was that he found Ben guilty of having a weapon without a permit. He said that the shooting was accidental due to Ben trying to defend himself. Ben was put on a strict probation, and I was asked to keep Ben on the dock instead of being a driver until his year probation was up. The judge wanted Ben to be in some kind of custody during the day, and also prohibited from going out at night until his probation had ended. We did as directed and Ben's work schedule was as a daily dockworker under my and the dock foreman's supervision. Once again, the long arm of the law was redirected due to known connected influences.

Ben asked me to go with him to a bar in Harlem after his probation time had ended about a year later. He wanted his friends to meet me, because they wanted to meet the "white boy" boss who kept him out of prison. It wasn't a real good time for a white boy to be going into a Harlem bar at night in the mid-1970s. The relations between the blacks and whites were at a high turmoil at this time. But I went with Ben because he said he has my back, and everything will be fine. As I said, I liked Ben and trusted him, so I went with him.

When I went into the bar, he introduced me to a multitude of men in there and they all shook my hand and told me how much they appreciated my standing by Ben when he needed me the most. I went to this bar a few times with Ben over time, and never had any problems with anyone. Bottom line is, they were all men that I liked, no matter what color skin they or I had.

The Christening

We had our second child, a girl, "Cheri-Anne" in March of 1974. In the summer we had a quiet christening at a Catholic church, with a celebration to follow at our home in Montvale, New Jersey. A lot of relatives and friends gathered on the rear yard patio with the kids including our now five-year-old son playing on the rear grass lawn. Guys that were associates who also came were in the dining room talking next to a bank of six-foot high windows that ran the length of the wall overlooking the rear yard and patio. I was in heaven.

My wife, of course, came from a different lifestyle because of her father's business as an underboss of the Genovese crime family. But when we first got married and I was merely a carpenter, we went from apartment to apartment until we were able to purchase this home. The fact is that she would have liked to stay in an apartment or maybe eventually a smaller house if I had only stayed the man whom she married, instead of who I had become. Sadly, not long after this event, we separated and sold that house that we loved so much.

Back to the Christening celebration at our house. Anthony, at one time, drove a red Cadillac. But during this incident, Anthony was still "on the lam" living down in Paraguay, where he had escaped to. The Feds wanted him but, at that time, could not touch him, even though they knew exactly where he was. He had married a young woman down there and had previously claimed political asylum, although it made his bigamy official. So why would the FBI think that he was at my house with his red Cadillac two years later? Answer is, just to break my balls.

It's now 1974 and I had recently purchased a custom-tailored (beautiful) three-piece suit to celebrate my baby girl's christening,

153

after losing fifty pounds through dieting. We prided ourselves in the clothing that we wore and the jewelry we had, especially since I never had a suit in my life, until becoming associated with Anthony. It was very important for me to have a new suit for my baby girl's christening, as our clothing in general was an extension of who we were and who we were associated with, and how far I thought I was removed from my life of poverty. We could recognize guys who we were associated with, at a distance on a NYC sidewalk when you couldn't yet see their face, by what they were wearing. They were either "wise guys" or attorneys. Custom-made suits are visually different than rack suits sold in men's stores. We could also recognize police detectives or FBI by what they were wearing. It wasn't their fault. We were just making a whole lot more money than they were as underpaid police. If they could have, they would have had nicer clothing in most cases.

And by the way I've had a change of heart over the past forty years or so, toward the police, FBI, or anybody that serves our nation that way. They are all heroes, and I wish I could have become one of them, instead of being associated with the Mafia. And they are still highly underpaid for putting their lives on the line for our safety. The bottom line at that time of my life was that custom-tailored clothing and a large beautiful house gave this farm town boy a sense of pride that I had never experienced. I was only able to do it because of my involvement with Anthony and his position with the Genovese crime family, and, ultimately, his love for me like a son, and mine for him.

Since being a true atheist, I had no religion throughout my life, although my wife was a practicing Catholic. We had our baby girl's baptism at the Catholic Church my wife attended (no less than four times a week, with offerings). With a father like Anthony and a husband like me, she probably should have gone more. It was somewhat of a small group at the church with just the immediate family and the godmother, who we named our baby girl after. After the christening we had a large celebration at our house.

We were only twenty-six years old and I believe had one of the largest houses in the neighborhood, located at the top of a small hill with a large back yard that was at the edge of the small greenbelt of woods which separated our property from the house below. Our driveway and garage were located on the left side of the house where a dirt road adjacent to our property that also separated us from our neighbors on that side. On the other side of the property there was a tall full-length hedge that completed our rear yard privacy. I mention and describe this for a reason you will soon see.

Our house was a 2,200-sf single level that we purchased from a doctor whose wife was in a wheelchair. Consequently, all the doors in the house were three-foot-wide (including the closet doors) which suited me just fine because of my size. We had three bedrooms, two baths, and a large living room with a fireplace, a formal dining room, a den, a large kitchen, maid's quarters (that we used as a playroom for the kids, no maid) and a two-car garage. The living room was located along the front of the house and continued into the formal dining room on the rear of the house. The entire front wall of the living room, dining room and den had six-foot-high sliding glass wood Anderson windows, with electric drapes. This detailed explanation of the structure necessarily sets the scene in order to understand how and what occurred on this day of celebration.

I explained all of this to show the difference of lifestyle that I now was able to have verses a lifestyle of poverty I'd had as a kid. We even had very nice dinnerware, dishes, and crystal glasses, instead of the paper and Melmac plates that I grew up with. Life was great as far as things like that were at this time of our life and marriage.

There were probably thirty to forty adults in beach chairs and patio furniture out on our rear patio enjoying this private Sunday afternoon celebration party. Kids were having a great time playing in the rear yard. My associates from the city were showing up just to show their respect with a christening present which was always cash. Trust me, none of them would go out shopping for a christening present. I have to mention an exception of a gift from Johnny "Dio" Dioguardi. He sent us a beautiful two foot by three-foot, toy-three-ring-circus. It was filled with toy animals, a ringmaster, a trapeze with trapeze artists, and clowns. All of the figurines were perfectly shaped and dressed in circus garb, performing tricks. He had that specially designed and constructed and sent to us at our home while he was in prison. To this day I still remember how special that was.

Since we were all associated with or were known or considered criminals, it wasn't good to all be together for long, so they typically came for a short time and left. I was sitting in the dining room talking with some associates when the following occurrence took place.

For some reason I looked into the living room and staring through the windows, I saw a bearded, long-haired stranger, wearing a black leather vest over his bare chest. Right when I saw him, he started walking toward the front door. Offended by this man looking into my home, I immediately wanted to beat his head in for intruding on our privacy. When I opened the front door, I saw policemen behind their car hoods and others behind my front yard trees with rifles and handguns aiming at me. There were at least five law enforcement officers in the front of the house. The bearded guy was now looking into my son's room at the far end of the house.

I immediately knew why they were there when I opened the door but decided to play a "trump" card and yelled out, "Don't shoot, I'll get him." I acted like I thought they were there to capture this trespasser who looked like a criminal inspecting my home for a burglary. Since I didn't have a gun on me, I took a chance that they wouldn't shoot me. As I yelled this out, I ran down to the end of the house where this guy was and tackled him onto the ground. Thank God I wasn't wearing my suit jacket! We were surrounded by flowers as I sat on his chest punching him in the face, when several guns were pushed into my face with a demand to stop.

With guns in my face, I of course stopped, but acted like they were going to arrest him and crown me the hero who caught him. When I got up, there was a man who identified himself as an FBI Special Agent and told me that the intruder was a local plain-clothes detective. By the way, he was not a happy person and was trying to figure out what happened while two policemen were picking him up and holding him up by the arms. I believe that he deserved it then and still do. I now protect my privacy with a .40-caliber SM MP automatic pistol. I'm not saying that I would have shot that detective, and I hopefully never have to shoot anyone (except a terrorist). I'm saying that I will defend my mother, wife, kids, and neighbors with a vengeance if necessary.

I told the FBI agent that I thought they were after the guy who was looking into my home, and who did he think he was to be looking into my windows? That's an infringement of my privacy rights. What if my wife was undressed in there? Then I tried to hit the mutt again but was deterred by several cops grabbing my arms and moving him away. The FBI agent told me it was a good thing that I didn't hit him once I had been informed that he was a police detective. I told him that I didn't care who he was because anyone looking into my house without my permission or a warrant to do so would get his jaw broken, including this long-haired hippy-looking mutt. I don't think that detective liked me.

The local police had also been involved, because the FBI had previously informed them and my five-year-old son's schoolteacher and principal that I was associated with the Genovese crime family. The FBI actually had gone into my son's school and talked with the principal and his kindergarten teacher, trying to see if he had told them anything about my actions. Are you kidding me?! Stuff like that only made all of us hate the FBI and police forces more. And now everyone in town knew about me which was okay with me. But why did my completely innocent wife and kid have to be involved in any way? Neither one knew a thing except that I was a manager of trucking companies.

I then asked why they were here pointing guns at me and my house. I informed them that I had a bunch of innocent guests, including kids, who could be hurt. He said that they were here because they were looking for Anthony "Hickey" DiLorenzo, since his red Cadillac was parked in the driveway. I said, "Anthony's Cadillac?! Are you too stupid to know that there is more than one red Cadillac in this country? Anthony left two years ago! Do you really think that he would come here in his old Cadillac, to be caught by you f——ing idiots?"

Then he told me that the FBI guy who was in charge was around the house in my driveway…where they had set up their base of operations. Base of operations?! As we were walking, I asked if it really took all the state and town cops, and FBI to set up a base of operations to look at a red Cadillac. We walked along the front of the house out to the driveway where there were three other cops and FBI officers standing around. But not the guy who was supposedly in charge. I asked who and where he was and was told that his name was Weintraub (as I remember), who I knew was the head of the New Jersey FBI at that time. I was told he had gone around back where all the guests were. I knew darn well that if the head of the FBI was there at my house on a Sunday, it was no accident. They had been planning this raid because they knew about the christening since they had been tapping my phones for years. And they knew that I was involved in "hickey's" escape but couldn't hold me.

So I then walked around back, and I saw FBI personnel taking down the names of all the guests. Now understand this…people partying in the rear yard consisted of kids, family, and friends who were as straight as anyone could be. Most likely they were straighter than the cops and FBI on my property, back in those days. There were aunts and uncles who had never done anything wrong in their lives. They had never been arrested and quite frankly were there with reservations because of who I was and who I was associated with at that time, anyhow. Now, here they were being questioned by the FBI who was recording it all in their little notebooks, including names, addresses, and automobile plate numbers. It was like a bad joke! When I asked an agent where Weintraub was, I was told that he had gone into my house. My wife was standing against the rear wall, next to the entry door to the house (that led into the kitchen). She was standing there smoking like a chimney. She was, obviously, very upset and nervous. This poor young lady had spent a lifetime with an (absentee) mob boss for a father. Now on the day of our little girl's christening, she had to deal with more of the same because of me and my involvement. I was supposed to be a carpenter, not associated with her father.

I asked her if she gave the FBI permission to go into our house and she said no. She said the two men asked where the person was who owned the red Cadillac parked in the driveway. She said she told them that he was in the dining room talking to me (since she didn't know what had been going on with me during this time in the front yard). When I realized that they had entered without permission, I was livid! I went into the house and found two agents in my dining room asking questions to four of my business/trucking associates. When I went in, it was Weintraub who turned around and asked who I was. I told him he knew exactly who I was and to stop with the bullshit. I was the owner of this house. I asked him who the f—— he thought he was to enter my house without permission or a warrant? He said he didn't need a warrant and that I should take hold of myself since he was an FBI agent. He then said that they were here to inquire about the red Cadillac parked in my driveway. He claimed that he had permission from my wife to enter the house! I told him that he was full of shit! There were at least twenty people outside who were close enough to have heard what was said between him and my wife and she would NEVER give him permission to enter the house without first discussing it with me. I stated that I knew that he had never asked, and that he was full of shit again! Then I told him that I didn't give a shit if he was the president of the United States, he was in my house without my permission. I also told him that this whole stinking event had been planned far in advance, because he wouldn't just get up on a Sunday and say, "Let's go to Elwyn's house with armed local police and FBI agents."

What a f——ing idiot! And were they so f——ing stupid that you couldn't check to see who owned the car by checking the license plates. The Cadillac in the driveway was clearly just an afterthought to give them a "reason" for raiding my daughter's christening party.

To return the surprise, I grabbed both of them by their jacket lapels, quickly backing them through an archway and into the kitchen and I pushed them through the screen door out onto the rear patio. Cool, and lots of fun, but pretty dumb move actually. Throwing around FBI agents isn't exactly a thoughtful move. I definitely was not thinking about charges of assault on two FBI Agents. I really didn't give a rat's ass if it was right or wrong, I just wanted them out of my house. As I followed them out onto the patio, I was immediately restrained by a couple of FBI agents who were then ushering me toward the garage. Since I was six-foot-five and weighed (at the time) around 225 pounds (mostly muscle), I was able to deter my travel long enough to make a concerted request of my wife as I was being ushered along.

Everything happened so fast, and the poor girl was completely frazzled at the time, she probably doesn't even remember what I said, much less carry through with my request. I told her to call the Bergen Evening Record (which was the largest local paper in the area) and then the New York Times, and then the Attorney General of the Unites States. I asked her to let them know what had transpired at our home, involving the FBI and local police having guns pointed and ready to discharge around innocent people and kids, and entering our home without permission. She was too upset to hear me but when I said the Attorney General of the US, I saw Weintraub nearly turn green. At that particular time, it was well known that the FBI was having a pretty hard time with the Attorney General. This was a ridiculous invasion of privacy and outright planned harassment. In addition to that, innocent people were possibly in physical jeopardy because of all the artillery that was there. Plus, because I tackled and punched a local detective, those local cops who might have decided to protect their detective.

They knew that I was among those who had helped Anthony escape and had been up in Canada with him; however, they couldn't put me in the clink, so this was definitely a case of harassment. The story about their suspicion that the red Cadillac was possibly Anthony's was just that, a ridiculous story, and they knew it as they knew I knew it. In fact, Hickey's wife (my beautiful and wonderful mother-in-law "Lillian") had driven the Mercedes that we went up to Canada in when he escaped, and it was returned to the house since it was still owned by her.

Once we got around to the garage, they put handcuffs on me and two agents were pushing me toward an unmarked car (obviously Weintraub's vehicle), as Weintraub followed us. It was clear that this action was taken because of my violence toward an officer (actually three counting the mutt in the window). Weintraub then said that I could be charged with resisting arrest, assault on an officer and assault of bodily harm on two FBI agents. Weintraub then told the men to stop and take the handcuffs off me before I got into the car.

And no…they didn't read me my Miranda rights. This is 1974, I was lucky they didn't just shoot me "and then" charge me with assaulting an officer of the law. Then he tried to explain that they thought that Anthony was there because of the red Cadillac and entering my home was a misunderstanding. I told him he was full of shit again because they knew he wouldn't be so stupid as to show up at his daughter's house, for a christening celebration especially in his "Arrest Me Red" Cadillac, if he had still owned one. He tried to apologize without looking like an idiot in front of his men and local police, and he told everyone to leave. They all left like a bunch of Keystone Cops in a hurry to become invisible. He stood with me and two other agents. He walked me away from the other agents and offered me an option. If I were to stop the complaint to the newspapers and the attorney general, he would not arrest me on those charges. Duh! Of course, I agreed. What he didn't realize is that my wife most likely didn't even hear what I asked her to do and would never have called anyone, even if she did!

I didn't push the issue with the newspapers and the attorney general because of our agreement, and the bottom line is it would have been stupid to bring down any further heat on myself.

When I walked around to the backyard, my guests, family, and pretty much everyone was trying to leave, or should I say, "Escape!" They were saying goodbye and giving their condolences to my wife, for the obvious catastrophe and embarrassment in her life because of me and her father. This activity spoke clearly that everyone was frightened to death by the incident. I felt so sorry for all of them and especially for my poor wife. She had had a miserable life with her dad and now with a husband that had been a carpenter when she married him—not a believed-to-be gangster.

My sister walked up to me and told me that she had been curious about all the men she had seen during the day around the other properties. I asked, "What men?" and she told me that she had seen men in the trees that she thought were working on the neighbor's properties as arborists or nursery personnel. I asked her, "Didn't it seem strange to her that men were in trees surrounding the rear yard?" She explained that she had also seen men in the woods at the bottom of the property. Also, men in the side property looking through the tall hedges on the right side, and men walking along the dirt road in suits, which she thought was unusual. I asked her why she didn't let me know. She said that she thought it was strange, but she definitely didn't think they were police or FBI—just people curious about the party in our rear yard. What could I say? The problems caused by my lifestyle were not something that my sister or my family or "straight" friends could have or should have considered or known about. Additionally, I considered myself a person who knew what was going on around me, and obviously was too involved with my guests that I didn't even see what my "straight as an arrow" sister saw.

Some of the family did stay for a while and of course the entire scenario was rehashed and discussed. In fact, we've had many laughs about that event over the years. Those close to me now who were there then, understand what happened and why. It would be one party they'd never forget.

Hijack and the Strangler

One night after work I went to the bar to meet with someone. As I was waiting for him, I overheard a conversation between three guys that I knew. One of them was talking about how much money he had made at the racetrack. They were all laughing and sharing their profits in betting, when this one guy says, "I can't believe he was able to do this for the whole week." That's when I got into the conversation since they were standing right next to me at the bar. I asked what they were talking about. I was told that a veterinarian had been paid to drug certain horses so that the races were fixed. That's why they made all this money betting on the horses in Saratoga. I asked why I wasn't told so that I could have made some dough too. This one guy looks at me and said, "Because not every friggin' buddy could be in on it."

Now, this is toward the end of my involvement because Anthony is away and I'm the one making money. He's one of the scumbags scraping from the profits that I made, consequently stealing it from Anthony. They had been lying to Anthony that my trucking companies were losing money, so they could put their hands in the till. At that time, I had heard enough and punched this so-called associate in the face, knocking him down with a look of complete astonishment. He was considering trying to kick my ass but thought better since he knew that I had training in karate and would enjoy his attempt. This mutt wasn't a "made man" just like me, so the only recourse he had was to take the punch, challenge me, which would only mean that he'd get more. The other problem that I had was that I was working my ass off in trucking and dealing with the Teamsters Union while they were just taking the profits and leaving me out of something like this fixed horse race.

I decided to make my own side deal and would definitely be leaving the assholes out of this deal and the predicted profits. I had been tipped off that there was a semi-truck filled with Nikon cameras coming through town and I'd already found a guy who wanted to help me resell them. I was at the bar to meet with an acquaintance, Vinnie, who I had decided to include in this deal. He had been one of my bodyguards during a union strike. He was of small stature, but it was always a mistake to underestimate him and his abilities. A while back, I was having a drink with him in a bar one evening, when he got in an argument with a guy over some nonsense. This guy had two others with him, and they also joined the argument, calling Vinnie names. Not good! Now, Vinny is about a foot shorter than me and these men were all larger than Vinnie. Vinnie hauled off and clocked this guy in the jaw and he stumbled into one of his buddies before going down on the floor. With that the other two guys decided to get into it, one going after Vinnie and the other pushing me. That guy was hit in the face with a *uraken showmen* uchi, which is a strike to the face that breaks his nose and fills his eyes with blood typically obstructing his vision. I followed that up with a solar plexus punch that knocked the air out of him. He was no longer in the mood to continue and sat down on the floor. That's when I was able to see if Vinnie needed help. What I saw was Vinnie being hit with the band's microphone stand, straight to his head, knocking him out. The second guy started toward me with an attitude. I then kicked the second guy with a *mae-ger-age*, which is a front upper kick to the face, which put him down for the count. The guy who hit Vinnie in the head was coming toward me, when Vinnie came to. His head was bleeding like a faucet, but he started screaming as he jumped up. Now the guy who had hit him quickly turns toward Vinnie and is knocked on his ass by a Vinnie punch to his face. Then, Vinnie jumped on this guy's chest and started beating the crap out of him. I decided that I had better stop him before he killed this mutt, not that he didn't deserve a wicked beating for hitting Vinnie with the microphone stand.

We left all three on the floor when we walked out of the bar and went home. I offered to bring Vinnie to the hospital, but he said he was okay, and after what I saw him do…he looked okay to me to.

This is another example of "the fight in the dog, not the size of the dog in the fight."

Back to the hijacking of the semi full of Nikon cameras: We stole a car in New Jersey, changed the plates with another set we had stolen, and followed the truck until it was out of the Queens Midtown tunnel where we would cause a predetermined fender bender on Route 495. We needed to have the crash far but not too far past the tollbooths because we wanted to make sure the semi wasn't yet going full speed.

I was driving, and we had the fender bender with the semi by my lightly hitting his front bumper with the rear side of the car. The plan was for Vinnie to get out of the passenger seat as soon as we were pulled over to the side of the road. He would then go directly to the driver side of the semi, and after pulling his pistol (while trying to hide it from all the drivers going by) would tell the semi driver to get out of the truck. I'd quickly be backing the car toward them, but away from passing cars so onlookers wouldn't see us put the semi driver in the trunk of our (stolen) car. The plan was that the guy would get his semi-truck back later that day along with $500 for his troubles. He wouldn't be happy for sure, but I would also be keeping his driver's license, reminding him that I knew where he lived, so he had better forget what we looked like when questioned by the police.

Well, everything went wrong after the fender bender and pulling over to the side of the road. Vinnie had a cannon, not a small pistol that he could conceal. He pointed it at the drivers face, very visibly to anyone driving by while yelling, "Get out," at the f——n' truck driver. Irrelevant to him were the hundreds of cars going by while he's aiming his enormous pistol at the truck driver. He was tough but not too smart. Thank God there were no cell phones back then! I had also explained that he was to get a small handgun that could be partially concealed like a snub-nose .38 revolver. But I see a 357 Blackhawk with a six-inch barrel (cannon) in his outstretched arm and I felt like I was in a bad movie.

Then the driver said, "Kiss my ass or shoot me, but I'm not giving you my truck." He continued with, "I just got finished paying off this rig and you aren't getting it unless I'm dead." Now, we had agreed and made it really clear that nobody was to get shot or hurt under any circumstances.

Vinnie does the only thing that he knows how to do. He throws the gun on the ground and at the same time jumps up in the air and grabs the driver by the neck and jacket collar, pulling him out of the truck and onto the highway while he's strangling the poor idiot. Vinnie is screaming something like "Didn't you see the pistol, ya big jerk? I should have shot ya."

The next problem was that as the cars were honking their horns and steering away from running over the two men on the right-side lane of the highway. I actually found this so funny that all I could do was stand there for a short while laughing out of my mind, *How could I have planned this with a guy like Vinnie, and also wind up with a driver like this guy?* That was just how guys get pinched and do time in prison. But I had to do something. So I picked up Vinnie's freakin Cannon that was lying on the street, while he's strangling this guy. I walked around them, trying to conceal what I was going to do, and hit this poor driver on the head with the butt of the .357, nearly knocking him out. When there was a lull in the nearby traffic, we picked him up trying to make it look like we were helping the guy who was injured during an accident and brought him over to the stolen car's trunk. We put him as comfortably in it as we could, after sticking some money in his pocket for his troubles and hoping that he was not too injured. I had taken his wallet out of his rear pocket and removed his driver's license. I didn't want the driver to get hurt, and if I'd had more cash in my pocket I would have given it to him. Also, the cash was in a pouch and we both were wearing leather gloves, so that our prints weren't on anything. We knew he was okay because he started yelling as soon as we closed the trunk. I explained to him that I had his driver's license, and he'd better not say anything that would lead to our arrest or conviction because we knew where he and his family lived. That was a bunch of bull, because I would never have carried through on that threat, but he didn't know it! I told him to shut up and he'd get his truck back soon enough. I sounded calm, but this was really scary! Not only had we hijacked a truck but could be charged also with physical harm and kidnapping of the driver.

I drove the semi and Vinnie took the stolen car, with the driver in the trunk, to a predetermined place where we had already left another car waiting. It was in a deserted area in Elmsford. After I had dropped off the load of cameras and collected the sale money, Vinnie met me again at a predetermined place where we'd drop the semi and leave.

Vinnie got half the cash and after we'd safely dropped the rig and had gotten away from it, I called the police to send them to where the semi driver was napping in the trunk and where his empty semi could be found. Then, we went to the races in Long Island, where I lost a ton of money on a horse that I was given an assured tip on. I think the nag is still running to get to the finish line, now some fifty years later. That tip got a tipster a punch in the face, only because he assured me that this was a done deal, where the horses had been drugged again, just like the Saratoga races. I wouldn't have bet so much if he hadn't assured me of the finish. I also wanted to go to the track so that when I won a good deal of money, I had an excuse for the cash.

A few years later, I told my associate who owned the trucking company that the Nikon cameras were originally supposed to be delivered to, that I had hijacked the load because of the way that I was neglected on the horse race deal. He was pissed and I couldn't have cared less how he or anyone felt. And no one wanted to piss me off any more than I was, for not letting me in on the Saratoga horse race. The money that was continually being stolen from the profits that Anthony should have had a piece of, and the money I lost due to the bad tip on the horse race, was always on my mind.

Oh yeah! I forgot to mention that from that incident on, Vinnie was known as "Vinnie the strangler." We got lots of laughs out of that!

My Favorite Club...or Not

We had a nightclub that we used to occasionally meet at, called Ali Babas. It was located in a position of New York City and was easy to access. The club had food, drinks, entertainment, and beautiful waitresses scantily dressed. We usually had a somewhat private room that was a step or two higher than the rest of the main floor and bar, with beaded tassels hanging down as a kind of curtain between the rooms. It gave us some privacy, because the room was somewhat dark while the main room was bright.

One evening after all my other associates had left, I experienced an interesting incident that added to my reputation as being an angry and violent man when pushed. I was standing near the bar just talking to a waitress that I knew from being there so many times. As we were having a simple, friendly conversation this guy walks up and slips between us, facing me. Then he says, "Who the f—— do you think you are talking to my girlfriend?" I was totally surprised by the interruption and so was she. I definitely didn't want to back down from this nitwit, so the anger in me rose and I said, "Because obviously you're a complete asshole."

I shoved him where he fell over a chair winding up on the floor. Realizing he'd messed with the wrong guy, I thought, he got up and quickly walked out of the club. I returned to talking to the girl as if nothing even happened. Apparently, she didn't care either, because she said she wasn't his girlfriend. Then, I heard the door slam and turned to see this punk coming through the entrance door and coming toward me pointing a pistol straight at me. When I saw the pistol, I immediately shoved the girl that I was talking to away from me with my left hand, trying to get her out of the line of fire, which positioned my body sideways to the man with the pistol. Everyone was now screaming and running away from this scene. Within a few seconds, he fired and the bullet just creased me under my left pectoral. I didn't even know it! But apparently with the shove of the girl, and my attempt to get out of the line of fire, I tripped over a chair, and wound up on the floor.

This guy continues advancing toward me around some tables with his pistol out in front of him. He stood directly in front of me and pointed the gun at me. At this time, I had my hand on the bottom of a chair leg and swung the chair across my body hitting the gun out of his hand. He started to go for the gun when I grabbed him by the leg and made him fall in front of me. I got on top of this punk and beat the hell out of him until he was unconscious.

Now, during all of this (remember we didn't have cell phones back then), no one had called the police. But lots of people were on the move to get out and believe me, people in those days didn't want to get involved by being a witness. The bartender and all the help knew better than to call the police at this time because they knew who I was, and more importantly who I hung out with. I got up and dragged this punk by his one leg over to the bar. I told the bartender not to call the police because it was all over. I then put the man's leg at the knee joint on the foot stool platform at the bottom of the bar and jumped as high as I could, coming down on this punk's thigh, breaking his Femur in two. He let out a scream and fainted from the pain. I ordered a drink and reminded the bartender to refrain from calling the police. I waited until he came to, enjoying my drink. When he did, I told him who I was and who I was associated with, and that he had better not tell the police who did this to him. Then I kicked him hard in the broken leg again, putting him out again because of the immense pain. This punk took a shot at me while I was standing next to a woman, so I had no sympathy for him in any way. I then left and went home. It was in the late evening when I got home, and my wife was asleep. I cleaned up whatever blood that was on me and put a bandage on the cut. I threw out my shirt when I got to my office the next day and she never knew anything about this incident either.

How I Was I Able
to Get Out?

I have been asked hundreds of times how I was able to get away from being associated with the Genovese Mafia. That's a question that is asked because most everyone has heard that a man who leaves any Mafia that they were involved with has to hide, or if one chose to be an informant (a.k.a. RAT!) they'd be given "Witness Protection." The difference with me is that I was never IN the Mafia, as stated hundreds of times, especially during my testimonies. I was only associated because of my father-in-law, who was an underboss of the Genovese Crime Family. He brought me in under his arm (as they say) to originally help me get a job to support my wife, his daughter, and later our family.

I was found to be very good at managing people, dealing with unions, and making profits in the trucking businesses. He and I and other mafia members and persons who were associated (such as I was), met often, and made decisions pertaining to the trucking businesses and union problems. Part of that would also involve other trucking companies and the multiple airlines that gave freight to forwarding companies like Emery Air Freight, and Air Express International.

Everything discussed during any meetings or personal conversations had to be kept in secret. Some of my actions may have been unlawful but I was never in the Mafia, especially since I have no Italian blood or ancestry in me. Did I do things that were unlawful? Definitely! But my association was through Anthony, not directly with plans, action, or knowledge of the Genovese Mafia Family.

I was still a major part of the trucking business and doing collections at times for people who wanted to stay quiet because of their problems with the law. That is until Anthony's associates, who were stealing the profits that I was bringing in, wanted me out. They wanted me out because Anthony had now been caught and would be able to possibly see what was really going on, including their stealing from what he had built up. I owed my allegiance to Anthony, and they knew it!

In 1977, I was running a second trucking company called "Advance Trucking." It was located at the Air Express International building in Kennedy airport. They were the air forwarding company, and Advance Trucking did the PU&D (pickup and delivery) services from the airlines to the recipients all over New York. We picked up the airfreight from the multiple airlines, sorted it into specific trucks that had specific routes where the freight was delivered to. At the same time, they also brought freight back in for export.

The problem became the same for Air Express International as it was for Emery Air Freight. I did a good job with the trucking and making profits, so the forwarding companies were very satisfied with the service. However, human nature came in to stop the flow. Both companies finally realized that they were dealing with companies associated with or owned by the Mafia. After years of our trucking companies' direct owners coming to meetings with diamond rings on fingers, $1,000 suits, and new Cadillacs at least once a year, they both concluded that they were paying too much to have the delivery services, and went back to doing it themselves. They knew that we did it better than they ever did or could, but the jealousy factor came in. Consequently, we lost both of those big contracts.

When the Air Express forwarder canceled the Advance Trucking contract, I was told that there was no place for me in the organization anymore. Anthony was gone and so was I after many years of making them money. And it wasn't ME that blew the contracts with the airfreight forwarders. I could have been brought into other trucking companies over the years but was loyal until I was suddenly unemployed. And Anthony had no say since he was in prison. Forcing me out made it even easier for them to continue stealing from Anthony.

When I was released from Advanced Trucking due to their losing the contracts, Air Express International offered me the job of running the trucking for them. I took the job and did it for about a year. The problem was that in order to have me, I was offered and paid more salary than the man who was supposedly my boss. I felt this was deserved because he was worthless and knew very little about the trucking business. Consequently, we didn't get along and I told him to keep out of my business, or I would show the terminal manager that he knew nothing. Then, after about a year, the terminal manager was let go and a new terminal manager came in from Germany. Siegfried was a real piece of work.

At that time my wife and I had separated, and we'd sold the house. We split the proceeds and I bought another house in Ridgefield Park, New Jersey. I needed to move personal items to her new residence and to my new house. So I borrowed a truck over the weekend and moved the belongings, bringing the truck back on Sunday afternoon.

I had always been able to use any truck I wanted over the years, so I didn't ask, I just did it. I once was given a 747-airplane freight container (called and Igloo) from Pan American Airlines because they liked my services so much. And I made a, let's say, trade with the dock foreman. I put the Igloo on a large truck and delivered it up north to my father in Saranac Lake, New York. Which is about three hundred miles from NYC. He wanted to use it for ice fishing. He took it out on a lake near him (Lake Clear) during the winters and used it as a fishing lodge. He put a wood stove and chairs in it and drilled a hole in the ice to fish from. The hole had to be drilled because the ice there sometimes gets several feet thick. I drove back and that was that.

When Siegfried found out that I had used the truck without his authorization, he called me to his office. After a short conversation he fired me for using the truck without his permission. He handed me a decent severance check. I told him to kiss my ass and don't get up because I would gladly kick his ass, and that was the end of my trucking involvements.

I bounced at high end expensive nightclubs and discos in the evenings and worked as a carpenter during the day for a friend who owned a construction company. My wife decided to take the kids to New Mexico where my sister had moved to, to get away from me. About a year after she moved, I sold my house, and moved also. I hated being away from my kids and eventually wound up in California.

After selling my recently purchased house I packed a small eight-foot U-Haul and went on my way to Santa Fe, New Mexico to see my children. The only thing that I really regretted was leaving a girl that I loved on the steps of the house as I left. I wanted her to come with me, but she had a great job and her family was in New York, so she decided against coming with me. I had to go, because I missed my kids with every ounce of my body but leaving her was a horrible experience that left a hole in my heart for many years. She finally married and I knew she was happy, although I knew that she didn't love him like she loved me, and she knew I loved her more than he loved her.

I went directly to Santa Fe to see my kids. My wife had moved there because she would be near my sister who moved there with her husband in 1974 after the house that they had designed and had built was finished. Needless to say, my wife didn't want me to live in Santa Fe, since she moved there to get away from me. So I left for California!

On the way I went a little north and through Las Vegas, NV and wound up staying there for a week. During that time, I stayed at the MGM (which was later changed to some other hotel).

When I walked into the gambling casino, I immediately came to a decision not to gamble. I loved to gamble, but one look at all of the opulence and I knew that all of that had not been achieved with their loosing's. I never liked to be taken and gambling in casinos like that is nothing more than playing with the odds completely against you. I stayed a couple of weeks going to bars, primarily to discos where I danced with beautiful women and later went to my apartment with them. I threw Champaign parties with multiple waitresses, barmaids, and women that I met wherever I went. I had a ball, let's say, and spent most of the proceeds from selling my second house. I didn't care, all I wanted was to have fun, dance, drink, and be continually with beautiful women. I wanted to forget about my youth, my involvement with the Mafia, separating from my wife (who was also beautiful), and being away from my kids.

From Las Vegas I went to California and wound up in San Diego. I'll never forget when I first saw a place called Mission Bay. It was so totally beautiful even as I was traveling on a highway going past it. I had to stop and see it closer, so I pulled off and stopped at a parking lot. I went and sat on a picnic bench and absorbed the beauty of the beautiful water, seagulls flying in the air, trimmed grass, flowers wherever you looked, kids playing, and stillness in the air without the noise of congestion, only the sound of the birds and the kids. I sat there for hours, until I had to find a place to live.

I headed west and wound up in a city called Pacific Beach. It was also beautiful. The clear blue Pacific is far more beautiful than the cloudy green Atlantic (in my opinion). I found an apartment to rent and unloaded my possessions before going to a U-Haul to turn in the trailer that I had rented. The problem now was that after I rented the apartment for a month, I only had $80 left since I had blown most all of my money in Las Vegas. When I got to the Uhaul rental place, they told me that I owed a lot more money than I had because of my delaying the trip by staying in Las Vegas. I told them I didn't have the money, and could I leave the trailer and pay them when I got work. I was told that I had to keep the trailer until I could pay the extra cost, and the trailer would incur the rental fees until I returned it and paid everything. This reminded me of back when I was collecting on some risky money loans and the vig would continue to rise until the whole loan was paid off. Bad move on their part.

I went directly to the beach and put a hand-made "4 SALE" sign on the trailer. It wasn't there more than an hour before some guy came up to me and asked if I was serious. I sold it to him for $500 and he went on his way with the trailer. I didn't care in the least. The driver's license that I had in New Jersey was canceled. No one knew where I had gone to if U-Haul tried to find me. I got a California driver license as Chuck Elwyn not Charles Arthur Elwyn and never heard a word from U-Haul.

Well, back to my getting out of the involvement with the trucking associations. I got a call one day in my Pacific Beach rental from the main owner of the trucking companies that had screwed Anthony by lying about the profits I had made running the trucking companies.

He knew that I always kept good records of both of the trucking companies that I managed. They were precise, showing the weekly amount of freight the profits of the freight moved, over the cost of the salary and truck costs. When I ran the Emery Air Freight PU& D service, I quadrupled their freight in five years, and we lost the contract because of the same reason I explained about with Air Express. Too many diamonds, and new cars. I had five years of handwritten records that filled about six boxes that I had brought with me to California that were then stored in my apartment closet. He said that they wanted to sue Emery for canceling their contract and needed the files to prove that we had done a better than good job. I asked him what he was going to give me for the records. He asked me to bring them back to New York and we would talk about it. I responded with, "First of all, I'm not coming back to New York. Second, if I did, I'd probably have to beat the shit out of you and every other shithead that will be there. No, it would feel too good and I'd be put in jail when they found your fat ass in the hospital. Oh yea, the bottom line is, are you f——ing kidding, thinking that I would trust you? After a few seconds he asked if I would meet with a guy they would send out to talk with me. I agreed and met him at the San Diego airport the next day.

It was in the evening and I picked him up in my car and we started driving north on the Route 5 throughway. He was talking about how they needed the records and when they won the suit, I would get a cut. This guy was bigger than me. He talked like he had an Italian accent, but was a big Irishman with red hair and white skin. He slid over next to me and put his big hand on my neck and started putting painful pressure on my neck. He told me that I was going to do exactly what he told me to do. Then he told me to drive him to my apartment where he intended to take the records and fly back that night.

I asked him if he was told who I was other than that I ran trucking companies. He responded with "Yeah, I know you was a guy who collected and thought to be a tough guy, known as the "Indian." But I'm in charge now and you do as I say, or else," all the while squeezing my neck. I said, "Good," and then struck him with my right elbow in his neck as hard and fast as I could, knocking the air out of him and bending him over in intense pain. Still driving down the highway, I grabbed his neck and smashed his head against the dashboard three or more times, knocking him out. I reached over his bent over body to his door, slowed down to about fifty-five miles per hour and pushed his fat ass out of the car. I watched him rolling on the road in my rearview mirror until he rolled off onto the side of the road, thinking, "Goodbye now! I hope for your sake I never see you again!"

I went directly to my apartment and called my prior boss back. I told him that I had picked up his tough guy and we had a little talk, before I threw him out of the car while driving on the highway. "I did slow down to about fifty-five before doing so. Are you kidding me? Did you think that that fat ass, a supposed tough guy, would frighten or have a chance against me? Now you listen carefully and hear what I've got to say! I'm going to load all of the records into my car and drive to a place that I often go to. It's called Mission Bay. It's just off the Route 5 highway in Pacific Beach. There are round concrete open areas that you can put firewood into and start a fire. I often sit there with a bottle of wine and just enjoy the beauty of the water, the beach, boats going by and other fires all around the bay that is about a mile across. I'm going to go there with a beach chair and watch the files burn instead of wood, so that you can never use them, ever. I'll wait until tomorrow night so that you can make whatever plans you think you can make. I'll be on the west side to the south side end of the parking lot. And remember this! I will have my weapon with me if I need to kill any punk that you send to find me. And if someone does come and I live… I will find you and torture you while I give you blood transfusions to keep you alive. Now you make the choice, I'll be there, and the files will burn." I hung up.

I burnt all of the files while having wine and enjoying Mission Bay the next evening. THAT WAS THE VERY LAST OF MY INVOLVEMENT AND I NEVER HEARD ANOTHER WORD

FROM HIM OR ANYONE. Oh yeah, I checked the papers and found an article about how the police found a guy on the side of Route 5 in really bad condition, but he lived. I'd bet he still has a limp! I'll also bet that he never again sat next to someone and squeezed their neck to show his strength.

One of the truths that is learned on the street and in life (only most people ignore it) is that if a poor man steals a car, a wallet, or even an apple to eat because he is homeless, he is called a thief. However, if a rich man steals a company or an idea, he is building empires. The poor man is looked down on and punished with years of prison, and the rich man is respected and revered. It appears that the more that you steal the less you must fear, especially if you have the cash to prevent the punishment. In NYC the local cops (back then) were bribed to allow certain types of crime to persist, like prostitution, drugs, theft, gambling, money laundering, murder, kidnapping, bribery, and extortion. If the crime or infringement was larger than the available payoff or bribe, it had to go up the ladder of authority such as a police captain, judge, mayor, governor, or even a senator. The unspeakable could persist as long as there is a profit for everyone.

Anthony's Murder

After Anthony did his ten-year internment, he was released from the Ray Brook Federal Prison in New York. He then tried to get back in graces with the very men that he mentored for years, and businesses he made, as the underboss of the Genovese family. However, apparently since he had been away for so many years including his time in Paraguay, not one of his prior associates wanted to give up any part of the piece of pie he had previously built that they had obtained in his absence. Consequently, he became very aggravated and distressed by the lack of cooperation to help him gain any kind control over what they had, in my opinion, stolen from him.

The following is taken from *The New York Times* in 1988.

> When he was incarcerated in Ray Brook there was another Genovese crime family member there with him by the name of D'Arco.
>
> D'Arco made these statements that were later written in the news. The following is directly copied from the news report.
>
> In late 1988 DiLorenzo and D'Arco were both out of prison. Near the end of 1988 D'Arco encountered him on Prince Street in the company of Peter Chiodo, a capo in the Lucchese Family, and Raffie Cuomo, a member of the Lucchese Family. A week or so later in a restaurant in Manhattan D'Arco met DiLorenzo while he (D'Arco) was sitting with another soldier in the Lucchese Family and an associate of the Gambino Family. DiLorenzo started to talk busi-

ness to D'Arco, who asked him to step outside. DiLorenzo then asked D'Arco to introduce him to Carlo, a Lucchese associate who was a heroin dealer. D'Arco told him that "the last couple of guys" that talked about narcotics, "they whacked them." After this conversation D'Arco warned members of the Lucchese Family to stay away from DiLorenzo, believing that DiLorenzo was wearing a wire. D'Arco also talked to Ida who told him to tell the members of the Lucchese Family not to give DiLorenzo "confidence", i.e. do things together with him.

A little later D'Arco encountered Ida sitting with DiLorenzo at the Tazza di Café. DiLorenzo greeted D'Arco, stating that he knew him: "I go back with this kid, we used to hijack trucks." Ida was livid but sat "just with a little smile on" while DiLorenzo "kept it up for three or four minutes." Raffie Cuomo then entered the restaurant, greeted DiLorenzo as a friend, and left with him. Ida and D'Arco were alone together. Ida motioned to D'Arco to step outside and said to D'Arco, "Why they are giving him so much, you know, keep them away from him, from Hickey." D'Arco said, "I'll see what I can do." He was about to say, "It's your own guy. Why don't you keep him away?" but Ida said, "You know what we are going to do?" D'Arco did not answer him. Ida said, "We are going to whack him."

Anthony Hickey DiLorenzo as a made member of the Genovese Family had obligations to the Genovese Family; if the Genovese Family believed he was an informer it is likely the family would seek his death. It is equally unlikely that his death would not have been arranged by some other branch of La Cosa Nostra. The murder of DiLorenzo was itself an overt act of the conspirators.

The conclusion that Ida was a participant in a conspiracy to murder DiLorenzo and aided and abetted that murder is a conclusion based on the convergence of these pieces of evidence:

Ida, only later was a consigliere, but then a capo in the Genovese family, took specific responsibility to warn the Lucchese Family that DiLorenzo could not be trusted.

Ida told D'Arco, "We are going to whack him." "Whack" in Mafia argot now common-place in gangster movies means "kill." The "we" of this sentence must be understood in the context of the conversation as referring to the Genovese Family. A reasonable jury could under-stand this statement as a declaration by Ida that he had associated himself with this project of the Genovese Family to kill DiLorenzo. A further reasonable inference is that if Ida, only a capo, was privy to the project, he was expected by the administration of the Genovese Family to have a part in its execution.

On November 25, 1988, DiLorenzo was at his home in the town of West New York in New Jersey. In the early evening a jogger saw a man shooting into the front door of DiLorenzo's house. He also saw a car with New York license plates double parked in front of the house with a driver waiting. The jogger ran to call the police. The car was gone when the jogger returned from making his call. The police arrived at about 7:50 p.m. and came upon DiLorenzo shot to death in his backyard patio. The gun used to kill him was found on the other side of the backyard fence.

It is undisputed that the conspiracy to murder DiLorenzo was in furtherance of the racketeering enterprise constituted by the Genovese Family.

Ida, also known as 'Little Jimmy' and 'The Little Guy,' was convicted after an eight-week trial of conspiring to murder Genovese capo Antonio 'Hickey' DiLorenzo in his New Jersey home in November 1988. Prosecutors say Ida and his fellow wise guys thought DiLorenzo was a government informant and were worried over DiLorenzo's 'erratic' actions. Among other charges, Ida was found guilty of supervising the operation of two gambling dens at the festival, conspiracy to transport stolen construction equipment and conspiracy to defraud the federal government. Evidence showed that Ida defrauded the City of New York and various charities by under reporting the money generated from rents paid by vendors at the annual eight-day festival. The 57-year-old mobster faced a mandatory prison sentence of life without parole. Ida was also convicted of plotting the murder of another Genovese associate, Ralph DeSimone, who was also suspected of being an informant. DeSimone was found dead in 1991.

Here is my opinion on what has been said about Anthony being an informant. It is only an opinion, because I was not involved with Anthony in any way at the time of his release from prison or his subsequent murder. At that time, I was a California licensed contractor designing and building custom homes in Lake Tahoe. But I knew this man and loved him like a father. Not a father-in-law, but a father who at one time I believed loved me like a son. We discussed all kinds of things when we were together alone, but never anything directly concerning issues with the Genovese family, other than trucking and union problems. He would never give up anything on anyone no matter what anyone else says. It wasn't in him. He was brilliant and loyal to the Genovese family in every way. The men who claimed he was an FBI informant were just trying to clear a path to get him out of the way.

The problem in my opinion, was that he was not reaccepted into the family again as a working member. He was struggling for acceptance and related income. I heard rumors when I was in San Diego about how he was so frustrated by how he was being ignored or even denied as a family member in New York. He had sacrificed and built up a large organization that supported many other members. Then, they just stole it all from him.

I seriously doubt that he was even talking to members of other families as stated by Ida and D'Arco. The members of other powerful families such as the Lucchese Family would never discuss anything with a member of the Genovese family. They would be writing their death certificate with the Lucchese Crime Family. I stand by Anthony and in my opinion, he was killed because he was a bother to guys like Ida and D'Arco who didn't want to share the businesses he had started and built. That was already evident! Why didn't they bring him back in after his release from prison? That's really easy to explain. These guys are criminals and criminals only think of themselves or they wouldn't be criminals.

Listen, it's no surprise to me that members of the same crime families kill one another. That's a given! But he would and never could be an informant or a rat or a traitor to anyone in the Genovese family. That's a lot of BS.

METAMORPHOSIS

Joy with Me

It's June 1979 and (as mentioned earlier) I was living in Pacific Beach San Diego. My niece, Joy, was visiting me for a week and were at the beach together the whole day. Playing in the ocean waves, baking on a blanket in the sand, enjoying the ocean breeze, the waves, the sun, the clean air, the palm trees, and each other. She is a special, wonderful girl to me. She's 17 years old, beautiful, and talented in so many ways. She played the guitar and wrote poetry that was beautiful. She was physically fit and trim, with long blond hair and a smiling beautiful face. She had just graduated high school and it was her last day with me before going home the next morning.

We were leaving the beach and I was packing up some remaining items, while she started for the car before me. As she went up onto the concrete "boardwalk," three bikers who were sitting on the wave break concrete wall stepped out in front of her blocking her walk. They were talking to her, and as I was then walking toward the boardwalk myself, I could tell that she was startled or frazzled by their interruption and apparently what they were saying to her. I put down the items that I was carrying and hurried toward her. When I reached her the three bikers looked at me when I told her to go to the car. I walked past the bikers, catching up to her and asked her what they were saying. At first, she told me that it wasn't a problem and "Let's just go home." I pried more because she was pretty upset, and she finally said that they were commenting on how she filled her bikini, and how much they liked her, in so many rude ways. I gave her the keys to the car, I told her to keep going to the car and that I would catch up in a minute. I was in San Diego and was trying to change my life, but the old me came through again. Especially since they were abusive to my niece Joy.

I returned to where the three men were standing, and they turned toward me and one of them said, "What the f—— do you want?" With that I grabbed the tallest, who I believed to be the leader by his long hair and slammed his face down on the concrete walk by falling to my knees. I put my other hand's thumb into the eye that was not being rubbed on the concrete along with the side of his face. Then I yelled out to the remaining two guys that if they moved toward me in any way, I was going to pull this mutt's eye out before beating their heads in and doing the same to them. The guy on the ground was yelling, "Get back, get back, don't come!" With that, they stayed away. I told the two of them to get over the concrete wave-wall down onto the sand immediately or I'd pull this guy's eye out. They obeyed and jumped over the wall into the sand.

That's when I rubbed this guy's face into the concrete a couple of times and explained that that was my little niece that they were way too rude with her or any girl or woman. I went on about why I wanted to break their scrawny, dirty necks and then stood up. I told them that if it ever became necessary, I would kill all three of them. The guy on the ground got on his knees but did not stand until I left. The other two also just stayed where they were and didn't attempt to follow or jump me while I was returning to get the blanket and stuff that I had dropped, when I ran to Joy's defense. After obtaining my personal effects I walked past them and to my niece Joy, in the car. As I was walking away keeping them in view, I told them that I lived in town and came to the beach often, should they want to review and possibly retaliate for this incident.

I did see them a few times after that incident, but never had any further problems with them. Eventually I never saw them again. Possibly that they realized how much I loved my niece. Although, probably because they moved further south toward Mission Beach, where they could hassle other young girls without any problems from me. Fact is that they were like most supposedly-tough-guys in the world. All talk and no action. Lots of tattoos and clothing that reflects some sort of gangster association, but without brains or courage.

Today we have these young men who wear their pants down so far from their waists that one can actually see either their underwear or the crack in their asses. It's actually pretty disgusting to many and especially to me. I can't imagine that young girls like this disgusting style. The way this style of dressing started was due to gang members being locked up. The fact is that when you are arrested the first thing they take from you when you're put in jail, is your personal effects along with your belt. The belt can be used as a proficient weapon.

In fact, I have used them as weapons more than once when I was a kid. I was shown how to use a belt as a weapon from the father of a girl that I was dating when I was only seventeen years old. I think he showed me how it was done so that I would fear his tactical abilities. He was a former marine that was in Special Forces and looked it. It did make me very aware, but she was way too beautiful to prevent my, let's say, attention. Back then we wore what were called Garrison Belts. They were thick and wide and had a large belt buckle. If you needed to protect yourself. You wrapped the belt around your hand and left a length with the buckle unwrapped, which when swung was used as a very effective weapon.

Getting back to the belt being taken when one is incarcerated, when a gang member or anyone gets out of jail, they are given their belt back. But a trend started in Las Angeles, where the newly released person would not put the belt on as they walked out to meet their friends outside the prison. Consequently, their pants were falling down as they walked, and it became a sign of being a gangster. Hence these other nitwits have imitated their look trying to *appear* tough.

Another thing that has taken off with the youth of today is tattoos. When I was a kid and hanging around on the streets of New York. I was often in the presence of gang members who would go and get tattoos. They would want me to go and I did but never got one. I used to tell them that a tattoo was way too personal and could or possibly would be used as an additional method of identification. I reminded them that I was six-foot-five tall and about 225 pounds. That was enough of an identification as far as I was concerned. I definitely didn't need a dragon on my neck or on my arm to help someone identify me if I was doing something illegal.

Later when I was in association with the Genovese family through Anthony, I was advised of the same reason for not getting one. Anthony had a tattoo because he got one when he was in the Army, defending our country during World War II. Later when he became a criminal and was incarcerated, he never added any because of the same reason. In fact, I can't remember anyone who I was associated with that flaunted any tattoos.

When I see an obvious gang member or motorcycle gang member with tattoos all over their body some representing not only the gang that they are associated with, but where they had done some time, I think to myself, no wonder they did time. Or if they are a criminal type, they are going to do time because the tattoos make them easily recognizable.

Our identification that expressed who we were associated with was wearing the best and most expensive shoes, custom-made suits, shirts, and ties. And we exuded an attitude of courtesy and respect, unless that attitude was changed with a challenge.

Joy's Death

It was only weeks after Joy visited with me and returned home to Santa Fe, New Mexico, that she was killed. It was July 1979 and I was acting foreman and sometimes superintendent for a multimillion-dollar remodel to a Vons grocery store in Palm Springs, CA. I did twelve of these remodels starting at 7:00 a.m. on a Sunday and ending ten days later. We had about one hundred men with different specialties like electrical, concrete, carpentry, glass, metalwork, general labor, and a lot of other men and subcontractors as needed. We worked in revolving shifts on a twenty-four-hour, continuous work program in order to complete the job at a set time.

It was a Tuesday evening July 10, 1979, three days into the remodel, when I was told that I had a phone call. How anyone got the number for this grocery store to contact me was alarming unless it was the construction company that I was working for. I went into the office and said hello. I can't remember who was on the line, but someone in my family told me, straight out, that Joy had been killed in a car accident. I nearly fainted! I fell to my knees and, for the first time since I was a very young, cried my eyes to dryness, sobbing uncontrollably. Joy was not only my niece but a lot like a baby sister to me since she was born when I was twelve.

I immediately told the other men on the job that I was leaving to be with my family and my niece Joy. I flew to Santa Fe, NM where she had lived with her mother, father, and brother since she was about twelve. She had been reviewing her opportunities for college since she was an excellent student.

That day she had visited my wife (since we were not divorced yet but separated for a few years) who also had moved to Santa Fe with my son and daughter. After Joy left from their visit, she was headed north on the apartment complex driveway and stopped her car at an intersection on a main road. As she was waiting for traffic to go by on the main road, a truck driving westward on the far side of the main road made a last minute, fast left turn onto her street. When the driver did that, he cut off another large truck heading east that hit him broadside and threw his truck onto Joy's car, killing her immediately.

The police said that the driver who had caused the accident by making an illegal turn in front of the other truck was not intoxicated. This was actually pure unadulterated bullshit! There was a car that had been traveling behind his truck that had told the police that he not only was swerving while driving, but they saw him throwing beer cans out of the window. They were from out of town, and consequently weren't a witness that was believed or called to be a witness. For whatever reason the police lied to protect this drunken murderer.

We had a huge funeral for Joy with hundreds of her friends and family present. Again, I was on my knees crying during the entire event. When they had lowered her into her grave and put a tarp over the open hole everyone left. I couldn't leave because she was in that open grave, alone, and not covered with soil that would hold her body forever.

I was waiting at the grave when a man from the graveyard or funeral home walked up to me, and I asked him why Joy had not been covered yet. He told me that the men who did that would do it before the day was over. I nearly went mad!

After he left, three of Joy's friends from school walked over to her grave and saw me. I asked them if they knew where they could get a shovel for me, so that I could cover Joy's grave with the dirt that was standing next to the grave. They said they would get one and returned with a shovel for me after a short time. I took off my suit coat, my tie, my shirt, and my jewelry and threw it into the grave with Joy. I didn't ever want to wear any of it again in my life, because it would immediately remind me of my Joy's death. I would have thrown in my pants also but most likely would have gotten arrested for indecent exposure. However, I did throw them away when I got to my sister's house.

I shoveled the dirt into her grave shovel by shovel, tear by tear, memory by memory, until her casket was covered, and all the dirt taken from the grave had been put back. In my mind, this would protect her from any further invasion or hurt. I couldn't stand to think that she would be by herself in that grave, exposed without covering.

I am crying as I'm writing this just remembering her, remembering how much I, and all of us loved and still do love her, and that horrible day when she was alone. I can't help but cry whenever I share this story with anyone even to this day, forty-two years later.

Trials and Tribulations

If you return to the LORD with all your heart,
remove the foreign gods and the Ashtaroth
from among you and direct your hearts to
the LORD and serve Him alone; and He will
deliver you from the hand of the Philistines.
—1 Samuel 7:3

Once I changed my life, all my stolen jewelry was removed from me by being stolen from me when I moved to San Diego. That theft helped to wipe away my past, my wealth, my Ashtoreth, and gods. He delivered me from the Philistines (my Philistines that I should never have been able to get away from) and changed my life. Even more importantly, He showed me that my associations and lifestyle were with the Philistines (criminal) and it was important to get away and change my life to know Him.

It's was 1981 and my niece Joy's younger brother Adam had come to visit me with his cousin in San Diego. They were thirteen years old and were having a great time together at the beach, in the waves, sailing on Mission Bay, and doing all the fun things an uncle does with his nephew in beautiful San Diego.

They'd heard about a place called "Black's Beach." It's a beach where you have to climb down a vertical cliff 350 feet to a beautiful white sand beach that's so secluded, you don't need to wear a bathing suit. The short version is a "nude beach." I quickly became a favorite uncle. Actually, I am the only uncle, and we loved and love each other then and today. The only negative from our fun day at Blacks Beach is that Adam's cousin, who is a fair skinned, red-haired kid, should have put on sun protection…especially on his butt. He didn't!

I told him several times to do so but he neglected my advice. He went home with a badly sun-damaged butt! His mother asked me why I didn't put sunscreen on him. Guess what I said? "There was no way I was going to rub ointment on his ass, under any circumstances!" We still all laugh at that experience, thirty-nine years later.

I mention this because we had several conversations during Adam's time about what was going on with his mother, my sister, back home. I was aware that there was a real problem with the young man who had killed my niece. I explained earlier that he had been drinking and he also made an illegal drunken turn that caused Joy's death.

However, he was never brought up on charges, nor was his driver's license even revoked, which would have made it clear that he was, in some way, responsible for his actions that killed my niece. His being charged would also have given my sister, brother-in-law and Adam some sort of finality or peace that he was punished in some way. I might add that this young man was known to be a problem to the police in other ways besides his bad driving record. Yet the fact that he killed my niece was ignored. At the time or should I say year that I am writing this, we were informed that he was killed in a violent manner, just like he lived. Forgive me God, but I was very happy to learn that not only he was dead but killed in a violent manner.

My sister and brother-in-law had been trying to at least get his driving privilege taken away for some period of time, by bringing it before the courts in New Mexico. They had hired an attorney who was representing them, but each time the court decided to do nothing.

It was only after several court appearances that I learned that the judge showed his frustration with my sister and brother-in-law's efforts to find closure, by revoking and reinstating this guy's license back in an intolerable way. He slammed his gavel on his desk, stating that his license was revoked; he followed that action directly by slamming his gavel again with a statement that he remanded the license. Handing over the driver's license to this guilty offender in the same minute he had taken it away. This made it clear to me that it's a good thing that I wasn't there! I'd probably still be doing time. It's my opinion that this scumbag judge and the police somehow were associated with this punk's family.

I began having nightmares about Joy's death, and the man who had killed her by his recklessness. I also felt that because of the arrogance and pure stupidity of this worthless judge's actions, Joy's family was suffering from emotional abuse.

In my nightmares, Joy's brother, Adam, told me that the driver who killed Joy was coming to his family's property (which is a very private many acres) drunk and screaming out to them, "I will kill all of you, and nothing can be done, just like with your daughter!" In this terrible dream I could see how upset and scared my sister was each time he came. I guess that due to immense stress all of this was causing me, I actually came to believe that these dreams were reality. I started believing that this was really happening.

The Plan to Kill

My belief was that after this last and final court hearing, the guy that had killed my seventeen-year-old niece was feeling powerful about the court outcome, instead of remorseful, and I could not bear it. Actually, we have no reason to think that he was ever remorseful, but now I realize that I didn't know him enough to say what he felt. Then I didn't care what I knew about him, other than what had happened due to his drunken recklessness. Again, my belief due to my nightmares, was that he was coming to my sister's house in the middle of the night, drunk, and yelling out to them inside the house, "I'll kill all of you if I want to." Of course, he left before they could see him and verify to the police that it was him. All I could do is feel their pain and fear, even though I didn't realize, at the time, it wasn't true.

Whether or not these things were true, I decided that I needed to kill this drunken vehicular murderer. So two weekends in a row, I drove from San Diego to Santa Fe, nine hundred miles straight through, not telling anyone about where I was going, or anyone there that I was there. I left after work on Friday afternoon and drove straight through to Santa Fe, to "tail" this kid and to observe his actions and movement patterns. I followed him from his house in the mornings to different friends' houses, and once to a park where he met other men and played some ball, always going to a bar in the evenings.

He was nineteen when he killed my niece and now, he was twenty-one. He went to bars during the day, and at night he would go to two different bars or dance clubs, and I would wait outside until he went home, just observing his movements. The first time that I got any sleep was Saturday evenings when he went home to bed.

At the end of the weekend I would return to San Diego on Sunday evening, after following the scumbag, and then go directly to work on Monday mornings, so that no one would know that I had been gone for the weekend. Even my sister and her family in Santa Fe were not informed of these excursions. I intended to do the same thing the next weekend, only with one important change. I was going to wait for him outside one of the bars that he frequented. When he came out late at night, usually by himself, my plan was to assault him, in a secluded place, on his way to his truck. I knew I could knock him out with one hard, purposeful punch, and then put him in my trunk. If the plan wouldn't work at the bar, I was going to run him off the road somewhere where it would not be seen.

On my return home, I intended to drive into a completely isolated area of the Arizona desert that I had scoped out on my two trips to and from Santa Fe. I would dig a hole in the desert, put a bullet in his head, bury him, and return home pleased that I had taken revenge in exchange for Joy's life and this punk's lack of caring.

The problem was, I realized later in life that this was not God's plan for me, and he orchestrated it so that I didn't kill this worthless punk, "Thank You God."

The Cornerstone

God made evil necessary because without it free will was impossible, and without free will there could be no growth, no forward movement, no chance for us to become what God longed for us to be. He made us human not robots. As horrible and all-powerful as evil sometimes seems to be in a world like ours, in the larger picture, love is overwhelmingly dominant, and, in my case, it would ultimately be triumphant.

That summer of 1981, I was involved in an extensive addition and remodeling of a church in Point Loma, CA. It was called a remodel because all that was left standing was part of the roof structure and support posts. Keep in mind that I was still an atheist. I didn't believe in anything like a God. When I hear people say that there really are no atheists, I say, "Oh yes, there are." My father was an atheist and raised me to be one too. I believed in nothing. I didn't care if I lived or died and I lived my life accordingly, in my youth and when I was associated with criminals. So as you can imagine, I hadn't spent much time inside of a church prior to that.

There was a young man who was working on the church with us named Troy. He was a long-haired, skinny, but muscular kid who was already married with a baby. Several times after work he would attempt to convince me that there was a God and that His son was named Jesus. Troy didn't drink, or take drugs, or curse, and he was a heck of a carpenter. He also was a heck of a surfer who would go surfing during lunch, right below the cliffs where the church was facing the Pacific Ocean, instead of eating. By the way…he became, and still is, my closest friend for thirty-eight years now, even though there are about fifteen years between us. Although, I eventually did become a follower of Christ, I don't believe that I ever shared this whole event and the repercussions with him. But he knows that he was part of my conversion to a belief and relationship with Jesus.

God puts people like Troy in our paths to help us to know the Truth, or at least want to know the Truth and start looking for it. He has used me many times over the years to help people to know the Truth of His love, and His desire to have them with Him after their death on earth.

I believe it was a Tuesday, when several parishioners and the pastor came to the job site where we were working at the time, at the front of the building. They came to request and witness the breaking open of the original cornerstone which was on the front corner of the church. Their purpose was to obtain the paperwork of the original structure which typically is stored in a cornerstone. Typically, before a cornerstone is set and sealed, the builder, owner, or, in this case probably the original pastor, puts documents/information about the construction, pastor, times, and the people in the cornerstone vault before closing it up permanently. Usually it's sealed with a granite or marble slab on the front. As I remember it, when I broke open the marble front of the cornerstone, we only found some newspaper clippings and some other inconsequential things. Everyone was rather disappointed because they had expected more documentation including a copy of the original plans!

After that, everyone left, and we continued our work by tearing off the sections of stucco in the front of the existing church wall that held the cornerstone. This included not only the stucco but wire mesh and building paper over plywood structural sheathing that is attached to the wood framing prior to the installation of the stucco.

We proceeded along the front wall and as we had gotten about halfway across, when one of the men held up a galvanized pipe about four inches in diameter and about eighteen inches long with two end caps on it. He asked me what he should do with it. I gave him my crude New York answer directing him to either throw it in the trash container or stick it somewhere else. He threw it into the dumpster, and we resumed work.

After a while, however, something inside of me asked, "Why would a galvanized cylinder be located within the framing stud cavity with two end caps on it? It certainly wasn't meant for any plumbing. So I went over and retrieved it from the container, grabbed some pipe wrenches, and took off one of the end caps.

I found documents inside of the pipe! I discovered the very papers that should have been inside the cornerstone. They were the dedication papers that showed the contractor who built the original structure, the name of the original pastor, a set of plans and the date that the structure was dedicated as a church.

When I read the date, something inside me became intensely alert, because I was not one who believed in coincidences. To me, there was always a cause and an effect. When I saw that this church was dedicated on the exact day (and the year!) that I was born, June 3, 1948, I immediately wondered why I was the one to find the documents. Not just to find them! But the fact that they were in a closed container, within a framing cavity with stucco on the outside and plaster on the inside, such circumstances would have and should have kept these documents from "ever" being found! And why? Why would someone put these papers where the probability was that no one would ever find them?

Why me? I was now thirty-three years old and had traveled about three thousand miles from my home in New Jersey to be the one who found the papers that showed that the church that I'm help- ing to build was originally dedicated on my exact birthdate!

I didn't say anything to any of my co-workers other than explaining that I was going to the pastor's office to give them to him. I felt that they would just say it is some coincidence and convince me of the same. I for some reason wanted to hear what Pastor Bringman thought.

When I spoke with the pastor, I told him of my revelation con- cerning where the papers were discovered and the facts of the date. He suggested that God had put them there for me to find, so that I could "believe in God." He said that only a miracle from God could have put them there, because we both knew that there was absolutely no explanation or reason that any person would do it. The papers of the church dedication would be placed so that they could be found in the cornerstone and appreciated, not hidden in the framing wall cavity.

It was at that moment and during the ensuing sleepless nights that I found myself entertaining the, then, *ridiculous* thought for the first time in my life that there *could be*, possibly…a God! I had three days of thought and consternation about what to do. I hated this kid with all my heart and wanted to end his life on earth. But I also had never killed anyone, and now started to have a conscience concerning my intended actions.

I never returned to Santa Fe to kill that worthless lying, punk that killed my niece.

The Search

Because of the miracle God created for me, I went on a continual search for the truth about the existence of God and His son, Jesus. When the church construction was completed Pastor Bringman asked me to attend the church on the first Sunday reopening. He explained that I would experience the love between the parishioners, the deacons, and he wanted me to meet his wife. The interior of the sanctuary was in the design of seafaring Norway Viking. There was a large Viking type boat hanging from the vaulted ceiling over the choir section located in the rear of the sanctuary. The pulpit where he gave his sermons on God's Word was a front section of a ship that he stood in looking over the parishioners. There was a full-size ship's "binnacle" with a compass in the center of the raised front platform that represented a vital directional navigation since the Bible was read from there before the congregation. I was asked to read a passage from the Bible to the church members from that Binnacle on the first Sunday, before his sermon was given on that passage.

That Sunday in church started me on my search and I began attending church each Sunday. I also attended the Bible studies given by Pastor Bringman on Wednesday evenings. Before long, I was asked to be a deacon who was labeled the property-deacon, obviously because of my construction knowledge and ability. I designed and constructed a fenced in area playground for the children, with swings, ladders, crawl through tubs, platforms with slides, and a large sand box, with a sign that said Joyland in respect commemoration of my niece who was killed.

Although I went to church and Bible studies, I didn't actually find God in my life until I moved to Lake Tahoe, California in 1987. I was brought to a Calvary Chapel Church located in a high school auditorium in Truckee, CA. When I first walked into the auditorium from the hallway, I saw that everyone had both their hands raised in the air. Believe it or not, and this is the truth! I immediately thought that there was someone who was holding a gun on them and had told them to get their hands in the air. I walked in cautiously looking to see where he or they could be, and if I would be able to make a defense or attack. It took me a short time (while still expecting to see a man with a gun) to see that they were just singing and praising God. I later learned that the Bible tells believers to lift up our hands in the sanctuary and bless the Lord. You'll find this in the book of Psalms (Psalms 134:2).

Another main difference I found at this church was how the Bible was taught. I would never take away anything from Pastor Bringman's lessons because he was a great pastor and teacher that I learned a lot from. However, the Calvary Chapel method of teaching was, "Simply Teach the Scriptures, Simply."

It didn't take me longer than a month to go forward and receive Jesus as my Lord and Savior, by becoming a born-again believer in Jesus. It also took me less than a month before I was baptized in Donner Lake by my pastor Brian Larson. I remember praying to God just before my water baptism, for God to remove and prevent all the Demons that I knew were holding on to me and affecting my life actions. We stood in the water and the pastor asked me of my belief in Jesus and we said a prayer just before I was submerged. When I came out of the water, I distinctly remember how clean I felt. Not physically clean but cleansed from my sin and knowing that the demons that had been with me all my life were gone. You may be asking yourself, "Demons? What do YOU mean by demons?" They are what guides us towards sin, and I had many.

It wasn't long after that that I became involved with the church as a teacher in the toddler department. I have always and still do love being around and playing with kids of all ages, especially toddlers (two to five) and also infants. What innocence! I hear people especially new parents call the toddlers at the age of two, the terrible twos. I always correct them and explain that they are the terrific twos. Because they are now old enough to really begin thinking on their own, which is why they act so crazy to us, but demanding their independence since they are having new thoughts that are inquisitive, adventurous, experimenting and discovery. I love being around them because of those traits.

Keep in mind that I'm six feet, five inches tall and now about 255 pounds, with long hair, a full beard in the winter, which typically is from the middle of September to some time in May. When new couples come to church with their toddlers, they come into the kids' room and have to hand their child over to ME. Someone always had to be there while this would be happening, so that they could assure them that it was okay to leave them with me.

As the toddler teacher I was always reminded to follow certain procedures with the kids. First was to sit in a circle and share a section of the children's Bible stories with them. Sometimes twenty or more kids! Good luck with that! Then we could all play together with the kids' toys, bikes, etc. An old New York expression comes to me. "Fagedaboutdit" that ain't happenin'. When I was alone with the kids and everyone else had gone to hear the service, we played. An example is sometimes football with a nerf football. Just throwing it around and once it was caught or picked up, run like crazy. All the while the kids trying to catch the one with the ball, screaming like crazy. That is until someone comes in and tells me to quiet it down because it's too loud in the sanctuary. We did for a while, but their children, not counting me who is totally a part of all this with kids climbing all over me. And making them do flips with their hands under their spread legs while I grab their hands and flip them in the air. Talk about fun and noise, I loved it and did it for a few years here at the Santa Fe, Calvary Church.

I explained in an earlier section that I am now single again during this time for about two years. So I usually sat in the rear section of the seating where I could see most of the parishioners, and the pastor, Brian Larson. There was a woman who sat several rows in front of me that always caught my eye. What I loved was the way she worshiped God. With her hands held high, and a raised voice while singing praises to the Lord.

I remember saying prayers while sitting there that went like this. Dear Lord, please give me a woman like that. Because I know that a woman who loves you so much is the only kind of woman who could love and forgive me. I later found out that her name was Wendy.

She was seeing a man, Dave Cronin, who I was also a friend with. He was a known hero who piloted a United Airlines 747 going from Hawaii to Australia. The plane had just taken off from Hawaii for a short while only getting to around twenty-two-thousand-feet in elevation when a forward cargo door blew out. It resulting in a gaping hole in the side of the aircraft that caused two rows of seats being ripped out, killing nine passengers.

Additionally, two of the plane's four engines were inoperable. But Dave Cronin was able to not only turn the plane around, but also landing it safely at the Honolulu airport about twenty-five minutes later saving 346 people. When the plane was inspected, they found, that in their opinion, that the plane never should have been able to turn around to get back to Hawaii. Dave was a deeply religious man who gave all glory to God for the miraculous piloting event. I felt it necessary to mention Dave, not only for his heroism, but mainly because he gave all glory to God, not himself. Every time he was in the news or even on the Johnny Carson Show. He continually gave all glory to God. This is what God expects of His followers.

Well, one weekend, I saw Wendy who I had met and spoken with once in church. She was alone, so I asked her where Dave was. She told me that they had decided to not continue to see one another. I immediately said: Are you doing anything on Tuesday night, I'd like to take you to dinner. LESSON: YOU SNOOZE YOU LOSE! She said yes and we were married about six months later and this year is our twenty-ninth wedding anniversary. Yes, because of God in our lives and our/her strength in Him. I learned during our courting that she thought that I was married because there were always kids around me or in my arms.

We both decided to be youth group sponsors. Besides meeting with them on a Thursday night weekly basis we went on several road trips with them. A man named Eddie Van Eck created a play including the acting and the stage design that portrayed evil as evil and God as love. It was absolutely amazing! Each year we traveled in a large bus owned by the church that brought at least forty kids and four adults to different prisons, youth reformatories, homeless shelters, and churches through the west and also Mexico. We experienced many people changing their lives by accepting Jesus as their Lord and Savior after this presentation by these teenagers. I could probably write another book with all the events, accomplishments, and amazing times while we were part of the Truckee Calvary Chapel youth group.

These kids were like pseudo children to us because of the time spent with them and the love they had for God by giving their time and talent to hopefully bring people to know and accept Jesus as their Lord and Savior. In fact, I am still in communication with Lindsey Nelson who lives in Ohio, who was a teenager in the Sun Seekers.

Work-Related Ministry

I started a program to fight against the typical attitudes of the men working under my supervision while either building new homes for my own business or for other contractors. On work sites there was always music playing during the work hours. The problem was that the men typically wanted to hear the music of the current era, such as hard rock, Hip Hop, Pop, or even Rap. I allowed their type of music to be played until the lunch break when I would insist on Christian music whether they liked it or not. As the supervisor or owner of the business, I wanted to listen to my desired music, which was of course Christian music, but I did not force it to be on all day, only in the afternoons. What happened many times was that it started conversations at lunch or even after work where some men wanted to understand why I was a Christian. That at times led to some men coming to our church and a few becoming believers in Christ.

In fact, it was years later when I had a call from a carpenter who had been working for me while building a home in Incline Village, Nevada. He told me that he had just recently received Jesus as his Lord and Savior after he had moved to and was living in Oregon. He thanked me for sharing my thoughts and decisions at the job site and for playing Christian music in the afternoons. He said that those periods of music and my sharing stayed with him all through his time while working for me, and after he had left. Then one day he decided to go to a Bible teaching Christian church in Oregon, where he received the Lord Jesus and became born again. I thought, "Now, there's a conversation I will never forget." Not because I am anything, but because God again used me to save another soul, which is the action that God wants from us as Christians.

Never Forget

Truckee with four men hassling a teenager and my reaction.

My acceptance of Jesus into my heart is not only what gave me eternal life with Him, but also what changed my life from what I was, to who I am now. I don't want to imply that I am a perfect person in any way. Only that His life in me taught me to look at myself, trying to continually improve who I am in efforts be a better person, to see my sins, and to love others.

My present wife of twenty-eight years now, and I were looking at a *60 Minutes* show about men and women soldiers dealing with PTSD syndrome and its symptoms. After the segment we looked at one another and came up with the same conclusion. Even though I was not in the war, I show many of the symptoms due to my involvement with crime figures way back in the sixties and seventies. At times I suffer from sleeplessness, nightmares, irritability, depression, anger, and flashback memories. Sometimes just coming out of a doorway I'm compelled to look around first. I often feel cut off from others, I lose interest in things that I used to care about, I get anxious, jittery, or irritated and I struggle to stay focused. I'm certain these problems are exacerbated by the fact I can't forget about those days of my life for the past forty or even fifty years.

Wendy often tells me, or tries to remind me that I am a new person. I am a changed man who is not like the guy I used to be. So I should release guilt associated with my actions. And while I know that she is correct, they are still part of my past and my subconsciousness and it's very hard to shake off.

I prayed that I would be able to get rid of my old violent self. In 1990, I was a California contractor who was doing design and construction of new homes in the Lake Tahoe area. At this time, I was definitely a "born-again follower of Christ Jesus." He had changed my life, and I was trying to change more every day. In fact, I had recently taken my second wife back despite her infidelity, because my heart was open and full of forgiveness. Sadly, she had played the harlot again because she had found someone new to screw. I now feel sorry for her, because I believe that she just suffered from insecurity. She was very pretty and although I often told her she was, she may not have been so sure. Hence, when some man fawned all over her, she got the boost she needed and succumbed to his advances.

At the time of this second adultery she claimed that I'd become a "religious fanatic," because of my commitment to Jesus. I was also trying to teach my stepdaughter and her sister's daughter, who was in our charge, the Truth. Apparently, I was a fanatic because I would read God's word and have devotions with her and the kids. Anyway, "Goodnight, goodbye, and good luck," as I used to say...and actually still do. So I became single again and did nothing but study God's Word (The Bible) in the mornings, go to work during the day building houses that I designed at night, and lift weights for hours after I got home. Then, I'd study God's Word and pray before going to bed. I was content, peaceful, and happy!

Then, I was put to the test! It was winter in the high Sierras in 1990. I'd been working on a house in Lake Tahoe and driving home in my pickup truck in the higher mountain altitude of Tahoe Donner, Truckee, CA. There are two ways to get to Truckee from the lake and since I was building a house on the west shore, I was taking the route from Tahoe City or Route 89 River Road. This route goes past Alpine and Squaw Valley ski areas, directly into the west end of Truckee. The Route 89 ends at a stop light that intersects with Donner Pass Road. (Yes, this is where the Donner party was during their famous winter in the Sierras). If you've lived there, then you know just what had happened. If you don't know, then look it up. It's part of our country's history.

Upon coming to the light at Donner Road, I started to slow down because it was snowing extremely hard. Believe it or not my truck was a two-wheel drive, despite living in an often-snowy area, and I didn't want to skid on the road. Well, a car behind me carry-

ing four men, sped up started to pass me on my right and sue
whipped in front of me in order to make the left-hand turn
Donner Road, at the light. Turning left would lead them to Route
highway that goes over Donner Pass continuing through Sacrament
and ending in San Francisco. I slammed on my brakes fish tailing all
over the road, stopping just inches shy of hitting their car.

I knew these guys were not from around Truckee because it's
a very small town, and I had never seen them before. So (I know, I
know... I use the word "so" way too often, get used to it) I assumed
that they were heading for the highway to get home. Then the old
me, the road-rage-before-I-found-Jesus came out! I suddenly had the
urge to beat the living hell out of anyone stupid enough to get out of
that car, while I was screaming and calling them names. I was livid
over their careless and reckless driving, so I decided to confront these
four mutts.

Then the new me, urged by Jesus, took over as I started to open
my door to confront them. I realized that these guys probably were
skiing all day and were on their way home down the hill. I also knew
that they had nearly created a crash due to their ignorance and may
also have a few drinks in them. Additionally, since they were not
from the mountain area, they may have not realized that they had
to make a left turn so soon and consequently cut in front of me. We
have all done it! So I closed my door and actually remember saying a
prayer for their safety on their way down the mountain. I asked for
their safe ride home and for forgiveness for my almost uncontrolled
anger that may have resulted in violence. And in my mind, hospital
stays for them, and incarceration for me.

The light changed and they turned left and traveled in front of
me for about one thousand feet. They then slowed down and pulled
over to the side of the road, hassling a teenaged girl that was walking along the side of the road. I knew her, because she attended my
church, and I also knew she was only about sixteen years old. I was
stopped behind them when I saw the windows go down on both the
rear and front passenger side, and they began to heckle this kid. Then
I saw that she was trying to walk away from them and had an expression of fear on her face. Their car slowly pulled forward as they tried

ak with her, about what I had no idea, but surmised it wasn't
.. She had come to a pile of plowed snow that prevented her for-
rd walk, and the snow was deep on the side of the road, so she had
 stop. They had pulled their car up to the pile of snow, preventing
her from continuing. They were probably just playing with her, but
I could see that she was very nervous.

That's when I pulled around them and stopped on an angle
preventing them from going any further. Two strikes, I only used to
believe in one! However, they didn't even know that I had stopped in
front of them. Because all four of them were leaning toward the open
windows, laughing and harassing this kid, when I got out and started
pounding on the driver's window, I startled all of them.

Understand this! I'm now a contractor with a thick beard and
a ponytail under my baseball type hat. I'm six-foot-five and carry
about 265 lbs. of solid muscle. And with all the clothing to keep
me warm in below zero weather, while I'm out framing a house in
the snow and ice down by the lake, I probably looked even bigger to
them. Consequently, not one of these guys considered getting out of
their car, which was good for all of us.

So the driver asked me what I wanted. I respond with, "Open
the window!" He asked again, "What do you want?" So I told him
that if he didn't open the window, I'd break it with my fist, pull him
out of it, and pound his face into the ground. He opened it about
two inches. I told him, either you open this window all the way, or
I'm going to break it and do what I said, along with anyone else who
would like to get out and discuss it with me."

He opened the window all the way and I leaned into it and
proceeded to lecture them about harassing the teen girl and nearly
causing an accident with me at the light. I also explained that we look
after our kids in this town, and I wasn't happy about them harassing
one of our teenagers, and neither would anyone else in this mountain
town. I went on about how they should get their asses straight out of
town or should get out of the car and we'd discuss it in another manner...like me breaking their heads and sending each of them to the
hospital for a stay. Meanwhile, the girl has walked away safely, while
I'm giving them the options with words that I shouldn't have been

using (hence, the old me). They decided to not get out of the car and all apologized for their actions, and vowed to go straight down the mountain and get out of my town. So I moved my truck and let them get on their way.

But as I was getting in the truck I was leaning toward the center and I saw myself in the rearview mirror, and I noticed my baseball cap. The front of my cap read, "Praise the Lord." God hit me like a bus, making me realize that all the time I was cursing, screaming, and challenging these guys, they were reading "Praise the Lord" on my hat.

It's not what they thought of me, because that wasn't the issue. The issue was that since I was wearing a hat, I obviously claimed to be a follower of Christ. What would their reaction be toward Christians, or, worse, Jesus, due to my actions? I was and am supposed to be an example to and of Jesus. He is the epitome of love, patience, and forgiveness! I certainly had not portrayed him with my actions toward these guys. He would not have wanted me to challenge them with anger and curse words.

I'm not sorry that I stopped and challenged them for hassling one of our kids or any kid as a matter of fact. We should all be on the alert to protect the young and innocent. However, what I should have done was confront them without the yelling and cursing and threatening. I could have said something to the effect of…if you continue to harass this young girl, first I will stand in your way with all that I am. And I will see to it that you are confronted by our local police. They would have done the same thing by not choosing to challenge me, and I wouldn't have insulted my faith and my God. Or another option would be to take off the hat and give them a beating for their actions. ONLY KIDDING, ONLY KIDDING!

This was a lesson that I never have forgotten. Now, understand this! Have I made mistakes since then? You can bet on it! But I still try never to be a bad example as a believer in Christ that would possibly keep anyone from knowing His truth and love.

Truckee Years Later

I was headed toward my home in Tahoe Donner one day coming from a job in Incline Village, Nevada via Route 267. After going over the mountain from Kings Beach, the road turns into a long stretch of open road that has long curves and height changes that alter the ability to see ahead at certain spots. I was near the middle of that stretch, following several cars, when all of a sudden, a Mercedes convertible came whipping in between me and the car behind me. There were several cars ahead of me, going the speed as we approached one of those long sections of curving in the road.

The Mercedes was right on my bumper. I have always hated tail-gaiters! Back in the day in New York, I would slam on my brakes, jump out, break the driver's window if it was closed, pull him partially out and punch him a few times in his face. Not that I was frustrated or angry about other things but because I needed a release. The problem with tailgating is that it's a form of intimidation. I don't like anyone trying to intimidate me then or now. The difference is although I still want to do exactly that to teach someone not to tailgate, I don't.

So this idiot decided to pass me and several other cars while approaching a big curve where he cannot see cars coming at him, and they won't be able see him on the wrong side of the road going sixty to seventy miles per hour. Consequently, he forces two cars off the road that were in the other lane driving toward him. I'm in my contractors' truck with cars in front of me but was able to see all of this as his car disappears around the curve.

Needless to say, I'm livid! He came very near to creating several crashes and obviously didn't care in any way. Miraculously, when I got to town and made the left turn onto Donner Pass Road, I see him getting out of his convertible which was parked along the boardwalk. I quickly pulled over and jumped out of my truck.

He didn't see me do this because he was yelling at his woman companion still in the car. I ran up to him and swung him around by his shoulder and grabbing the front of this shirt with one hand, I started smacking him in his face with the other. He tried to stop me, but he was no match for my size, strength, and anger. He was obviously some rich kid in his twenties or thirties who expected no results from his actions. He's leaning back against the car trying to get further away, but I kept pulling him forward smacking him.

As I was beating this worthless punk, I was yelling at him for almost causing several accidents. "You could have killed this young girl," I yelled, pointing to the passenger in his car. While I am doing this to him there are people on the boardwalk, and others coming out of stores, watching. Again, bad move on my part, because it's a small town and nearly everyone knows me.

When I was satisfied that he had had enough and my hand was killing me from slapping him, I got in my truck and left. Not a good thing to do as a born-again Christian, I knew, but I felt good knowing that he deserved it. I will also bet that he will never, ever do that again. When I was pulling away from the scene, I saw the woman in the car, get out and start walking away from him and the car. Oh yea, there were people from my church that saw the whole thing. But didn't chastise me when I told them why I had done it.

"Men's Issues" and
Another Mistake

It was now 2005 and we were attending Horizon Christian Fellowship in Rancho Santa Fe, CA. I had decided to start a men's Christian meeting on Friday Mornings called Men's Issues. I had shared my testimony at several men's retreats and conferences, and I sought to avoid starting a Bible study, but rather to build a gathering of men to discuss personal issues that men deal with, hoping that these things could be (confidentially) discussed between one another. I hoped to share experiences and obtain (Godly) wisdom on how to handle the issues in a proper Christian manner. After each meeting we were to delve into God's Word and study what He ultimately teaches us throughout the Bible.

Consequently, I put the word out to friends and men at church and sat in a diner in Carlsbad, CA, for nearly two months of Friday mornings praying that God would tell men to come and be a part of the proposed group. If it were His will to do so. Then one Friday morning a man showed up (Matthew Argue) and the Men's Issues program began. The first and most important thing that we vowed was to discuss any and all issues with only the men attended the group. We couldn't even discuss our topics or one another's issues with our wives. It was part of a secrecy for the right reasons, not like I had been doing in my earlier years as an associate of the Crime Syndicate.

In about a week or two other men started to come (Rob Denny, Doug Cole, Allan Bettencourt, Don Plachon, Pierre Grimillian, and later Steve Clover). Several of these men who attended have shared that the reason why they had accepted Jesus as their Savior, is because of being present at a men's conference and hearing my testimony discussed and ultimately pray for each man's issues such as wives a how to please them, children, drugs and alcohol, work, unacceptab language, how to study God's Word, and in my case…anger. It was and still is a very productive men's meeting and even though I moved to Santa Fe, NM in 2010, it is continuing and although Pierre has left others have joined that men's group. The best result is that these men are very close in friendship and honest in their thoughts and concerns for one another. And although I am not in San Diego in order to attend the Friday early morning meetings, I am still close to all of them.

It took me a while, but in March 2018 I started a men's meeting in Santa Fe, NM. We have at times seven men who attend (myself, Rob Gibbs, Wayne Glazener, Steve Pierett, Arron Pierett, Jim Squires, and Jim Shannaburger). There is no label such as Men's Issues with this group, we just meet together each week early in the morning and discuss whatever issues we have, pick various persons or verses of the Bible to discuss in detail, and of course we pray for one another and our families, our pastor, people in need, and our country.

Both these men's meetings are beneficial to us as men, because we grow closer in friendship, and in our belief and understanding of God's will for us as Christian men.

Here's another incident that occurred around 2005 (I think)—a type of road rage. I was still living in San Diego to be closer to the airport than when I lived in Lake Tahoe area. I had stopped building houses and began a construction consulting business. All of my experience in commercial building in San Diego and custom homes in Lake Tahoe gave me a great amount of knowledge and ability to evaluate damages and the needed reconstruction of large loss damages to commercial and residential buildings. I traveled all over the US working for larger consulting companies, insurance companies and attorneys, evaluating damages due to fire, water, hurricanes, tornados and anything that necessitated damage evaluations.

This day I was driving along Route 5 to meet with some Christian Brothers for our Men's Issues breakfast. I was driving my 1963 Ford thunderbird convertible and consequently driving a little

er the speed limit of sixty-five. My top was down, and I was just
nding my own business. Suddenly, this pickup truck came up on
my tail so close that I thought he might hit my rare custom T-bird.
I was in the right slow lane and tried to wave them to go around me
on the fast lane, if they wanted to pass me. There were two men in
the pickup and the driver started hitting his horn and waving for me
to get out of his way, instead of his going into the faster lane, which
would be the normal and correct maneuver. This was just absolute
abuse, so I suggested that they pull over to the side of the road so that
I could find out what they wanted, or why they were in fact challenging me. I really wasn't in the mood for a fight as I was on my way
to Men's Issues. Additionally, on my sixtieth birthday, I pressed the
weight of 300 pounds. So at six-foot-five and around 255 pounds of
solid muscle, I thought that they would also be deterred from starting anything. But I was wrong!

We pulled over to the side and both the men got out of the truck
and walked toward me. I thought that they would just apologize or
explain why they were doing what they did and go on their way.
That's when the driver walks up to me and says, "Listen, Grandpa…"
Well he's in his late twenties or early thirties, and it took me about
one half of a half of a second to drive my fist into his solar plexus so
hard that it lifted him off the ground and onto his truck's hood. With
him out of the way I turned toward the second man who had already
backed up toward his passenger door. As I started toward him, he
called out to me, "I've got no problem with you."

I looked at him and said, "When this scumbag punk is able to
breathe again tell him to never underestimate an older man's ability
to kick his sorry ass! Also, I absolutely hate tailgaters and he should
have just passed on the left-hand side instead of breaking my balls by
riding on my rear and honking his horn."

This mutt was still trying to get his breath, when I walked back
to my convertible and continued to my meeting. Now again, here I
was thinking that I didn't do what Jesus would have me do when I hit
this guy. I contemplated my actions the entire way to the breakfast,
feeling badly about my actions. But then, I thought that there is a
time when one needs to defend himself and that was one of those

times. Tailgating without any reason, both getting out and coming toward me after they had obviously created the confrontation. And lastly challenging me with an insult. Well, I'll bet that this guy never, ever, called an older man grandpa with the intention of trying to back him down again.

When I went to our meeting, I shared the incident with my brothers in the Lord. I believe that they may still laugh when or if they ever think of that meeting. Not that they didn't think that I was totally wrong but that they knew me and appreciated my restraint in the incident. I also got a lot of praying for forgiveness.

I shared these three times when I became violent and angry, because I wanted to share that just because you are a follower and born-again believer in Jesus doesn't mean that you never sin again. The incidences that I have shared are only examples of my sin being violence. Believe me, as a human being we all sin. As my current pastor, Skip Heitzig says, "I'm not sinless, but hopefully I sin less." The difference, hopefully, is that our sins lessen in numbers. More important is that as believers in Jesus we are forgiven for our sins when we sincerely recognize and ask God for His forgiveness for them.

God and Bob

My wife Wendy and I moved from Lake Tahoe to Encinitas, CA, in 1998. A nice young couple (Bob and Molly Cote) who were soon to have a baby, moved across the street a few years later. When I saw Bob starting to move contents from a moving van I went over and gave him a hand with the move-in. At that time, I was fifty-two years old and still lifted weights (which I have always loved) and I had a weight bench, barbells, and dumbbells that I used daily, in our backyard.

One day while I was working out while listening to my Christian music and occasional pastors' remarks or sermons. Bob called out to me from over the side fence gate. He said that he had heard the clanking of weights from his yard and asked if he could come in and join me lifting? Of course, I was pleased to have him join me. The only caution I had was that he was in his twenties and solid muscle. I later found out that he had been a football player in college and still looked the part. I was definitely fit, but fifty-two, so I automatically wondered if we would have to change the weights each time, we changed positions. When we did work out with the same weights, I assumed it was because he didn't want to embarrass me. We immediately got along well and after a while I invited him and his bride to have dinner with us.

When they arrived, they happened to notice that we had several Christian plaques and crosses on the walls and fireplace mantle that immediately made them cautious. I am a fairly good Italian dinner cook, due to my years with the Italians back in the sixties and seventies, although I am not Italian. As we were sitting down at the dinner table to eat my favorite dish that I had prepared (puttanesca), Bob asked us for his forgiveness, because he needed to explain something.

We said of course! He then explained that he had been brought up as a Catholic and wasn't continuing in any religious practices. So would we please not get into any religion discussions or an attempt to convert them? We certainly agreed to be compliant with his wishes, and we had a really good time together getting acquainted and learning about one another during dinner.

Well, I agreed not to discuss our belief in Jesus during dinner, but there were other ways to bring up a conversation without directly moving into an unwanted, direct discussion. Which I was going to do! Why? Because as a born-again believer in Jesus Christ, we believe in sharing the Truth with others so that they can have the opportunity to achieve a life forever in heaven with the One True God also. In order to spark an interest, I instead put on Christian music over my exterior speaker system, while lifting weights in the rear yard together. It was just music, so he didn't complain or even make any kind of comment whatsoever. Day after day we listened to the pleasant sound of Christian music that in itself makes one start to think about what all the entertainers are saying in their lyrics. After a couple of weeks or months (I'm not sure), Bob started to ask questions concerning my belief and faith. We had many discussions concerning his years of disappointment with Catholicism, and of course the sharing of my testimony surfaced—the change from a criminal to a born-again Christian.

Then one day Bob asked if he could go to our church with us, to see what the differences were between Catholic and a non-denominational Bible teaching church that we were attending. He wondered why I had so drastically changed my life and was so committed to my belief in Jesus. Trust me, I was ecstatic about him coming with us, and he went with us the very next Sunday. He said that his bride Molly didn't want to come with us, so it was only him coming with us.

It was the very next time when we were lifting weights together that he said this to me something like this: He expressed that he was glad that he was now a Christian. After a short laugh, I asked him why he thought he was now a Christian. He answered because he had gone to church and liked what he saw and heard, which helped him to believe, and that hearing a Calvary Chapel pastor explain the Bible was a life changing experience from his lifetime of listening to a priest speak in Latin, and not understanding the Bible. I believe I had another short laugh and told him this: just because you stand in a garage doesn't make you into a car! Neither does just going to a church make you a Christian, which is recognized by God, not man.

He asked me, "Well then, what do I have to do to be a Christian?" I explained that there is a quote in the Bible by Jesus that anyone and everyone must follow in order to show your true belief in Jesus. It's in John 3:3, when Jesus says, "Unless one is born again, he cannot see the kingdom of God." Which I explained is confusing to everyone who is not a Christian.

Consequently, Bob also asked, "How does anyone do that?" I explained again what Jesus told a Rabbi called Nicodemus, when he was asking Jesus how anyone could reenter his mother's womb and be born again (John 3:4). Jesus answered, "Truly, truly, I say to you unless one is born of the water and the Spirit, he cannot enter into the kingdom of God" (John 3:5).

Bob then said how do I do that? I explained that one must first truly believe in Jesus, and then say a prayer from your heart with total faith that will tell God/Jesus that you really believe in Him. He asked to do that right then, right here. I asked him if he truly believed that Jesus was born of the Virgin Mary. Did he believe that Jesus died and was crucified for our sins, raised from the dead, and is now at the right hand of God? He said, "Yes!" I asked him to get on his knees and repeat after me. He repeated what was just explained above in prayer. When he was finished, I told him that if he really believed what he had just prayed then he is born again of the spirit and should also get water baptized as soon as he can. I explained what had happened to me as I came out of the water during my baptism.

My wife Wendy and I started praying for Molly as 1 Samuel 12:23, "As for me, far be it from me to sin against the Lord, by ceasing to pray for you…"

Here's the bottom line! Not long after that his bride Molly went to church with us and went forward to receive the Lord Jesus as her Lord and Savior. Bob is still a brilliant man who liked and likes to study. So after years of studying the Bible and attending chur 2008 Bob Cote became the Pastor of a church he started in a store in Orange County, CA. It grew and has continued to grow that his church had to be moved to a larger building in Rancho Sant Margarita, CA, where it is today twelve years later. The church is named "The Spoken Word Christian Church." Not only does he do sermons or teachings in that church but also online for anyone and everyone in the USA and other countries.

Bob, Molly, and their two kids (now adults), Ryan and Ashley are still our very close friends.

Nebuchadnezzar
and Satan's Hold

I was blessed to be present when Pastor Skip Heitzig gave a sermon on the book of Daniel. I had now moved to Santa Fe, New Mexico. This sermon on Daniel is found in the Old Testament of the Holy Bible. As usual I take notes not only on paper but throughout my Bible as well. In the beginning of Daniel, God talks about how King Nebuchadnezzar tried to transform Daniel and his three friends by trying to integrate them into his world by influencing their thoughts, food, drink, religion, and loyalty. Daniel and his friends were Israelites who were conquered and taken as slaves by King Nebuchadnezzar. The king tried to manipulate them (as explained by Pastor Skip) through *isolation, indoctrination, intimidation, and redesignation*. However, with Daniel and his friends Hananiah, Mishael, and Azariah, it didn't work!

First, they had to have certain qualities that would be suitable for the position that they were being trained for. They also had to learn the language and literature of the Chaldeans. Then they were supposed to be treated with the king's choice food and wine. There's the biggest trickery...because they are being brought from slavery to the palace. Their teacher (or in this case their master) was seeing that everyone conformed to acceptance of the blessings and improvements in their status. They were also forced to learn about and practice things that would make them more Chaldean than (their former selves) Jewish. Finally, their names were changed from those typical of the conquered Jewish nation from which they came, to Belteshazzar (Daniel), Shadrach (Hananiah), Meshach (Mishael), and Abednego

(Azariah). If they had adhered to the demands made, they wou... truly be "Chaldean."

As I was listening to the message and taking notes, I realized that these are the very things that I lived through when I was "associated" with the Genovese crime family. I also believe that it was the same method used by the NYC gang (The Park Rats) I ran around with as a rebellious teenager.

Isolation

This is how isolation applied in my case: take me from my home-
land (from a small apartment above a bar, to a large beautiful home).
Separate me from my family (step by step because of hearing about
my involvement with crime members). And the priest (that I didn't
have or believe in as an atheist) worship of their God (Satan).

How were we put into *isolation*? That was an integral, important,
and very evident part of the association. We ONLY associated with
each other…the pre-approved gentlemen and perhaps their family
or confidants. This did not just apply to business but also in our personal life. We only associated with others who were in the same boat,
to use the expression. Being in the same boat meant that if someone
started to talk too much, even if it was with those who were associated, the boat could sink. We knew not to rock the boat. We went
to one another's houses for dinner, parties or barbeques, birthdays
and weddings. We went out to restaurants together. We drank and
ate together not only as families but more often as just men, talking
business and then partying together, often into the early morning
hours. We'd sing together in a type of camaraderie with one another
after getting high on alcohol to Frank Sinatra and the like. I now
know, although I was naive then that we were in common worship of
Satan. I use Satan as an example because what we did was generally
wrong. You couldn't trust yourself with outsiders because one slip
and you could go to prison or end up dead in the East River. Very
soon after my involvement started, I spent less and less time with my
extended family who, quite frankly, didn't want to be around me.
The *isolation* was a must and a tactic for curtailing any mistakes, and
molding an associate into who they wanted them to be.

Indoctrination

Indoctrination—challenge everything I learned growing up—brainwash my thoughts on crime, give me a chance to make a whole lot more money that would challenge my worldview.

In the beginning I had to be indoctrinated into the Mafia culture, "The culture of crime." At the start I had to prove myself just to get a job. It took attitude, desire, fearlessness...and a baseball bat! After proving my ability to cross a trucking union picket line every day for work on the cusp of my association, I had to continue proving myself as a dockworker, then driver, a dispatcher, and finally the overall manager of two air freight trucking companies owned partly by a crime member. The indoctrination for all of this was acceptance and increased income, the best of food, restaurants, bars, nightclubs and (I'm now sorry to say) women.

While coming from the poorest family in our town with little of anything, I started to be enticed by the best of everything. Along the way I proved myself to be acceptable if not favorable in the act of collecting money loaned out but not paid back. As my responsibilities increased along with my abilities, the thought of leaving that life was unimaginable. I respected and admired the men who were in positions above me because I knew that I was climbing the ladder of being a successful businessman (and criminal).

Intimidation

Concession—make this so amazing that I wouldn't want to go back to who I was.

Along the way as my position with the crime family improved, so did the *intimidation*. When running the trucking companies there were many decisions to be made and actions to be taken, which were not legal, with other trucking companies and the Teamsters union. Whatever I knew could only be discussed with certain designated persons. The bottom line was secrecy so that if anyone "leaked" they would be trying to swim in the East River with concrete blocks attached to their feet. If you were a loudmouth or rat, better known as a "stool pigeon" you would have some lead placed in your ear with a .38 revolver, or a knife wound that went from your abdomen to your breastbone, before the swim. The longer you were in, the more you took on, the more you knew, and the quieter you became. It was just simple criminal semantics.

Redesignation

Anyone who was associated with or is a part of the family had illegal dealings and were redesignated by being given new "handles" (nicknames).

As had been discussed earlier, the underboss of the Genovese family was my father-in-law Anthony DiLorenzo. He was known as "Hicky." He came to NYC when he was a teenager from upstate NY, which was mostly farmland especially in the 1930s. So he was called the Hick! There was an associate who was called "Jackie the Nose." Need I explain? Some other *redesignations* were "The Sheik, The Brush, Moon, and the Indian." I was the Indian. It's explained in one of my chapters how that "handle" was given to me. It was originally given to me when I was a teenager because of the way that I fought.

Having a handle was important because you didn't use someone's real name in discussions, just in case someone like the FBI was listening. They knew our handles and used them at times when they tied you down and tried to convince you to talk about something or someone, with threats and physical persuasions. They could call out all kinds of handles, but you denied knowing any of them. The problem for them was that it wasn't your name, so even though they knew the real names associated with the handle; it wasn't legal and thus a problem for them because we didn't call persons by their real names. Our handles were commonly used but the conversations were always careful. Hickey didn't want my handle to be commonly used, because it was used only when it had to do with illegal activities, and not with my positions in the airfreight trucking industry. In fact, to my knowledge, my own wife never heard it used nor was she aware of it. I'm sure that when she reads this book, she'll be amazed at that and a lot more. The bottom line is that when you were known by that new name, those who knew you respected you for it.

totally believe what God's Word says about how ачhadnezzar tried to control Daniel and his friends *by isolation, octrination, intimidation, and redesignation.* The same techniques ʻe used to change, control, and indoctrinate men into gangs, crime families, and crime in general. Give a man who has had nothing and thinks he's going nowhere, the best foods, wine, women, dance, and protection, he may be changed and controlled. The difference between Daniel and me was that I chose to accept the changes, he didn't. Satan got to me until I met Jesus, but not Daniel because he always knew God.

AFTERTHOUGHTS

Adultery

Many of the men living this lifestyle committed adultery. I'm not about to say how many women were in my life when I was married to my first wife because my wife didn't deserve my adulterous lifestyle and doesn't deserve any punishment now. However, as I stated above and in the previous chapters, criminals had lots and lots of girls or should I say women in their lives.

What I need to say is that although I didn't believe in a God or Jesus Christ then, I do now. If I had known the TRUTH back then, not only wouldn't I have been associated with these men but wouldn't have been an adulterer who hurt and embarrassed his wife. But there is a God! And He decided to teach me a lesson concerning adultery.

After I had left the life of crime in New York and moved to San Diego, I went back into the construction business. I had remodeled a church in San Diego and after it was completed attended the church to see if I could find evidence to believe in God, because He had created a miracle for me during the construction.

I was standing in the church's meeting hall having coffee and talking to the patrons when this very pretty and might I say sexy looking woman in her twenties approached me. She walked up to me and said, "Are you seeing anyone?" I told her no, since I had no steady woman in my life although I always had a girlfriend. She turned and wiggled away with a very tight knit dress on that no man in his right mind would not notice.

Well, of course that led to our dating and very soon living together. After a while she wanted to get married and we did. We rented a house in a town called Claremont in San Diego, after moving from an apartment in Pacific Beach. We decided to attend a "Marriage Encounter." You go for a weekend and stay at a hotel together, being taught certain practices that will enrich, or in some cases heal, marriages. We went for enrichment, and I was so touched about the teaching that when we came out of the hotel at the end of the weekend, I stood there with tears running down my face because I was so affected and pleased by what we had just gone through. And I don't cry.

We then became a part of a group of couples in our neighborhood that met to discuss our marriages openly with the focus on what we learned from Marriage Encounter. We shared with one another so that we could learn from each other's mistakes or achievements. I actually enjoyed it.

It was just before Christmas when my wife told me that she had been sleeping with another man a few blocks away, because he reminded her of Harrison Ford. And she shared that she had been seeing the woman leader of the couple's group that we had been going to and sharing her adultery experience with her.

We agreed, very strongly that she should leave me, and we should get a divorce, so, we did. Lesson #1.

Now, here's the best part! We had been divorced for a few years and I was a superintendent building a huge project in downtown San Diego. It kept me very busy, all the time. I had my office on the seventh floor of the office building, while the interior was still being constructed. But the elevator was operable.

I was sitting at my office desk looking at some electrical plans when my ex-wife walks in looking like something out of a magazine. I got up and she immediately started crying, asking me for my forgiveness and telling me how wrong she was, and how much she still loved me. She also had a way of always getting what she wanted with her womanly charms. So we made love.

She asked if we could start seeing each other again, since she was sorry and loved me. There are actually two reason why I agreed. The first, of course, is that she was very convincing of her remorse. Then there was the fact that I had been going to church now during our years apart, on Sundays and Wednesdays, still on a quest to know God

I still wasn't convinced, but as I had said God had created a miracle just for me that put me on my search for the TRUTH. I was studying a book in the Bible called "Hosea." A synopsis of Hosea is that he was married to a prostitute and God told him to stay with her, forgive her, and love her. So since I'm studying this book in the Bible, on the same thing that I have gone through. I thought that it may be another sign from God for me to forgive her and take her back as my wife.

We dated for several months, then rededicated our vows and then moved into a house together again in Claremont. Don't get me wrong, she was exceptionally smart and had a great job running a mortgage company office. But when I had completed the building complex job, I decided that I had to move to Lake Tahoe which is an eight-hour trip and over five hundred miles north. The reason why I had to move is nearly another book. Let's just say the reason involved the IRS.

She came with me and left her job, while I started a (custom home and remodeling) design and construction company. We were there for about a year when she told me that she had been sleeping (I'd like to use another term but won't) with another man who made passes at her while she was at a drinking fountain. And guess what? It was right near Christmas, again, which has always been my favorite time of the year. She told me this over the phone. Lesson #2.

Bottom line is "Good night, goodbye, and good luck." I believe that God wanted me to experience what I had put my first wife through, by bringing this adulterous woman into my life. Have I forgiven her? Absolutely! Just like myself, she didn't know any better, and I hope she does now. But don't call me! Obviously, I don't mean her any harm, which is why I didn't use her name, and won't.

I found God, or actually he found and forgave me. I later met my present wife in Calvary Chapel church in Truckee, CA. We have been married for twenty-eight years and I love her more every year.

Marriage should be when a man looks after his wife and kids with whatever he can do without doing criminal activity. God says respect and think of Him first, then your wife, then the kids, then the work to support the wife and kids. It shouldn't be the other way around.

Heroes

I have had three heroes in my life. While every other boy in school was worshiping an athlete or later an actor, I found them to only be doing their job and nothing more. I still feel that way. I never wanted to get someone's autograph even when I was sitting across a table with them at Sardis, the Copa Cabana, or a friend's house in La Jolla, CA. A Joe Torre, Joe Pepitone, Micky Mantle, Frank Sinatra, Richard Burton, Sonny and Cher, or even Charlton Heston (who I really liked), never had me awed. Their presence only brought on thoughts like, "I wonder what are they really like? Are they rude? Are they sincere? Are they afraid? Are they trustworthy? Are they associated in some way? Are they good people?" What I did know is that they were doing their jobs well, and I had a respect for that. But I do have three heroes in my life that went way beyond doing their jobs well.

The first was a man named *Audie Murphy*. I used to see him in movies when I was a kid and somewhere read about his war/service record as I got older. He was so small in stature that he had a hard time getting enlisted into the Marines to fight for America during WWII. Finally, he was accepted in the Army and sent to Europe to fight the Nazis and defend our county and others.

His whole number of accomplishments is far too lengthy to put into this book, and his name, character, and reputation should be investigated and appreciated by every American who has lived during his life and after. He was and still is the most decorated WWII veteran this country has ever seen. He personally saved hundreds if not thousands of American soldiers' lives with his heroic deeds. And did them all with no regard for his own life, with a humility that one could see in his face when acting a part on the screen as a cowboy or in movies about his service oversees. He had started as just a man considered too short by others to be of any value, so they turned him away but turned out to be larger than any man I have ever seen or heard about, with exception of Jesus. His heart and his bravery and his sacrifice has shaped my life and should and could shape so many others. Whenever I hear a youngster say to me, "I wish I was your size," I share with them Audie Murphy and what he did with his size. As another great man, Winston Churchill said, "Never, never, never give in." The giant is only as big as you make him.

My second, but not less than Mr. Murphy, is *Mother Teresa*. Yup, she has also been a hero in my life since I was a child, even though being brought up as an atheist. My father used to tell us at the dinner table that hell is on earth because of all the pain and misery that we will go through, but heaven is when we die, because there is nothing, just bodies decaying, no feeling, no life, no pain, no disappointment, no misery, no after life, no nothing. And consequently I lived my life accordingly.

To quote Mother Teresa, "A few weeks ago, I picked up a child from the street, and from the face I could see that the little child was hungry. I didn't know, I couldn't make out how many days that little one had not eaten. So I gave her a piece of bread, and the little one took the bread and, crumb by crumb, started eating it. I said to her, 'Eat the bread, you are hungry.'

And the little one looked at me and said, 'I am afraid. When the bread will be finished, I will be hungry again.'"

Mother Teresa spent her whole life serving God and helping people all over the world. I had a person say to me recently, "She was really a rude and very angry person."

My answer was, "Oh, you knew her?" There will always be people who want to steal away credit from people like Mother Teresa, or even God and Jesus. Don't listen and don't believe the people who don't really know the truth.

When confronted with a situation where life or death was or could have been eminent, I certainly had some fear. But I saw my two options and went for it. If I achieved the goal, life would be better, and if I failed and was killed, then life would be no worse. How many criminals, gang members, wayward kids do you think feel like that. They may not think exactly that, but deep inside they really feel like that. "That's scary," for them and for us.

The third hero, again in no order of importance to me, is *Corrie Ten Boom*. This was a woman born in 1892 and died in 1983. She lived in Holland and was a watchmaker along with her father. She and her family were members of the Dutch Reformed Church. When the Nazis came into their country arresting and killing any and all Jews, she and her family formed an organization to help the Jews escape and they hid Jews in their home. After they were discovered by the Nazis for hiding the Jews, she and her sister and father were also sent to concentration camps where the Jews were incinerated. Her father and her sister died in the camps, but she continued to stand firm on God's word, helping fellow inmates until she was freed by America and our Allies. After that, she continued to help and love people to accept Jesus as their savior including the very Nazi concentration camp soldiers, who aided in having her sister, father and millions of Jews killed. She practiced forgiveness like no other human, other than Jesus. She wrote a book called *The Hiding Place*, detailing the events of her life in Holland and in the Nazi camp. If you haven't read that book, make sure you do! This woman was also a true hero!

I have also found that I have other heroes in my life. They are the men and women who defend our lives and our constitutional rights daily. They include the men and women who are in the military armed services fighting wars and defending not only America but also many other countries in our world. They include the men and women who are in the FBI, CIA, Secret Service, state and local police, firefighters, paramedics, and many other organizations that put their lives on the line, every day to protect us. They are heroes for me and should be heroes for every American citizen.

I was drafted for the Vietnam War when I graduated high school in 1966. When I stood in front of the doctors who were doing physicals on us, they were making lots of remarks in fun, because of my size and excellent physical condition. They said things like, "Look at this young man, he is so big that just putting him in front of everyone else will save lives, because of all the bullets he'll stop." We were all laughing at the things that they were saying, because it was all for fun and put us at ease, especially me, because I wanted to go and defend my country against the rising communism. My mother had written a letter for me to give to the doctors when I was being evaluated. She had stated that I had a damaged back because of the car accident I was in when I was fourteen years old. However, I wanted to serve my country, so I never showed them the letter or mentioned my back problem. But the problem was that one of the doctors looked at my feet and asked me what size shoe I wore. I had a size 16 and had to special order any shoes that I wore because of my size. He then said to the other doctor, we don't have any (army issue) boots large enough. Consequently, I went from 1A to 4F which meant I couldn't be enlisted into the army because of my shoe size.

This hunger to have more, no matter who it hurt or what the effects are, is what drove people like me and Anthony and others to continue in ways of crime. Each time we ate from that lifestyle, we needed to reassure ourselves that there would be more of it by never stopping what we were doing. Each theft or each accomplishment led to wanting more, with a fear that we didn't have any other options to be successful in life. Take Anthony for example. I use him as an example because I was a toad in comparison to the whale in the pond that he was. He wasn't smart…he was brilliant! If he had put his mind, body, and soul into achieving what he desired in life by means of honest gain, he would have been a billionaire. I'm sure of it.

What we as people don't know about life, is explained in another quote by Mother Teresa, "Don't be afraid. There must be the cross, there must be suffering—a clear sign that Jesus has drawn you so close to his heart that he can share his suffering with you."

A book that I'm reading is *Hope for Each Day: Words of Wisdom and Faith* by Billy Graham and wanted to share this quote with you.

"We cannot fully explain the mystery of physical birth, but we accept its wonder, and we accept the fact of new life. What is it, then, that keeps us from accepting the reality and wonder of spiritual rebirth—of being 'born again'? To those who have experienced it or seen it happen in others, it is just as real as physical birth. Just as surely as God implants the life cell in the tiny seed that produces the mighty oak…as surely as He instills the heartbeat in the life of the tiny infant yet unborn…as surely as He puts motion into the planets, stars, and heavenly bodies—so He implants His divine life in the hearts of those who earnestly seek Him through Christ. This is not conjecture; it is fact. But has it happened to you? If not, you are not only fit for the kingdom of God—you are cheating yourself out of the greatest, most revolutionary experience known to any human being. By a simple prayer of faith ask Christ into your life right now. He will come in, and you will be born again!"

I've shared my testimony (1 Peter 3:15–16—always being ready to make a defense to everyone who asks you to give an account for the hope that is in you, yet with gentleness and reverence) to hundreds of men and boys in several churches, prisons, juvenile detentions, men's conferences and retreats in CA, OR, WA, UT, NV, AZ and Mexicali, a Mexico prison, over the years, since being "born again." This is my reason for writing this book. The bottom line is that many men have come to believe in God because of my testimony. I have been contacted numerous times by men who have heard my testimony. They explained that they didn't believe that God would forgive them because of their sins. Then I was told that when they heard my testimony of my prior life and sins, and that I have been forgiven they realized that their sins were nowhere as great or as displeasing to God as mine were! Consequently, just like myself, they accepted Jesus as their Lord and Savior, getting forgiveness of their sins and becoming "born again."

Here is the prayer that I said, and my life was changed, and I was given hope for the future, love for others, and an insured place in heaven by God when I leave this earth.

I prayed this prayer with a knowledge that what I was saying to God, was the absolute Truth.

Dear God, please hear my prayer. I admit that I am a sinner; I believe in Jesus; I believe that He is Your son. I believe that He suffered, was killed while being hung on a wooden cross, and I believe that He died for my sins. I believe He arose from the grave and is at your side in heaven. Please forgive me for my sins and accept me into your Holy presence. AMEN.

Once I prayed to God to accept and forgive me, I was "born again." Born again, most people can't even fathom what that really means, because in our worldly knowledge it makes no sense at all. I had no idea what it meant, until I attended Calvary Chapel where it was finally explained to me. In the Bible, Jesus explains:

> "Truly, truly, I say to you, unless one is born of water and the Spirit, he cannot enter into the kingdom of God. That which is born of the flesh is flesh, and that which is born of the Spirit is spirit. Do not marvel that I said to you, 'You must be born again.' The wind blows where it wishes and you hear the sound of it, but do not know where it comes from and where it is going; so is everyone who is born of the Spirit."

> John 3:5–9

There is no better feeling than seeing God change hearts. He uses us, but only He can change us and accept us into His presence forever.

Psalm 16:18—"Pride goes before destruction, and a haughty spirit before stumbling."

Proverbs 16:19—"It is better to be of a humble spirit with the lowly, than to divide the spoil with the proud."

Where are you?

Epilogue

I need to share the truth about the kid that killed my niece Joy on July 10, 1979, and the judge that was part of the trial. What I had written in a prior chapter called "Trials and Tribulations" was what I thought the truth was until I had my sister Tricia read my first rough draft before going to a publisher. As I had also mentioned she was and is the educated one of the family that became a professor in a college in Arizona. So I wanted her opinion on my writing. After she had read the first draft, she sent me some observations that I needed to change or correct about Joy's death.

My sister informed me that the hearing before the judge and the resulting charges were totally different from what I thought and shared. I was living in San Diego when my sister and brother-in-law finally were able to bring this punk ass kid to trial by jury for vehicular manslaughter. Consequently, I never knew the actual truth until just days ago when my sister told me.

Here's the Truth about Joy

I personally refuse to use a person's name who has committed atrocities such as killing multiple people like the men did in Las Vegas Nevada, or El Paso, Texas. And so many more worthless inhumane beings like them because it seems to make them immortal in memories. Forget their names and be glad that they are either dead or in prison for the remainder of their lives getting the beatings that they so richly deserve. However, I wish I could put the names of this murderer and the judge, but I have been advised not to because of possible liable suits.

Joy's mother (my other sister) couldn't accept this punk mutt getting away with killing her eighteen-year-old daughter, Joy. So she got an appointment with a Santa Fe criminal prosecutor who, after several attempts, finally agreed to bring charges against this drunken murderer and bring him to trial.

My sister, Tricia, said that the trial was very painful having to listen to all the facts brought against this punk, while watching the cold, callous reactions of him and his parents. However, the prosecutor presented an amazing prosecution and one image that he presented has forever stayed in my sister's mind.

During the personal testimony of the murdering bastard, he stated that he made the turn in front of the oncoming traffic because he couldn't see due to the sun being in his eyes. He said the sun was setting when Joy was killed and with the sun low in the sky, it was right in the eyes of people (meaning himself) traveling down the right side of the street (heading west on St. Michael's).

When he said he couldn't see because of the sun, the prosecutor asked, "You couldn't see, so you just closed your eyes, like playing Russian roulette, and drove across three lanes of traffic hoping no one would hit you?" The prosecutor had made a powerful presentation of what the driver did just before having the witnesses from Arizona take the stand. They had come to Santa Fe to be there at the trial and be witnesses of what they had seen. They testified that they had seen the driver throwing beer cans out of his truck while he was driving and had said to one another that something terrible was probably going to happen. They helped to verify how this punk totally disregarded anyone else when he turned across three lanes of traffic to make a left turn which ultimately caused Joy's death.

The jury convicted him of vehicular homicide which was unheard of in New Mexico at that time. Then, later, came the sentencing! My sister explained how terrible and ridiculous it was because the judge wouldn't allow ANY TESTIMONY from Joy's family, friends, or the Arizona couple who had previously testified and had returned to testify again before the sentencing. The judge also wouldn't allow this punk previous driving record to be presented either, which included that he had hit a school security guard with his truck just months before killing Joy. And after the trial but before the sentencing, he also had been given tickets for running stoplights just after the trial.

The judge ruled that it was vehicular homicide by this kid and even handed him back his license, with no punishment whatsoever.

Now I know that I shouldn't be saying this! But I am so glad that I wasn't at that trial. I loved and love my niece too much to have just accepted the judge's decision over twelve juror's decision that he was guilty of vehicular homicide. Of course, both my sisters were crying profusely after hearing this horrible decision. And neither the judge, the murderer, nor his family cared one bit. I think that they knew he was going to go without any kind of retribution because they had either paid the judge or was a close friend of the family. How else could someone get away with a jury verdict of vehicular homicide and get absolutely no punishment.

Back then in the eighties, I was still pretty much on the edge and not a follower of Christ. I believe that if I was present during the judge's refusal to give a proper judgement. I would have gone over to the kid who killed my niece and twisted his neck, killing him on the spot. Then I probably would have gotten to the judge and have done the same to him. I know, I know, how could I have done that? It's called years of anger, violence, and training in Japanese karate. After killing the kid in front of everyone why not kill the crooked judge also? Why on earth would a judge make such a careless, cruel, and unjust decision? I, obviously, feel that it was solely based on friendship and of course money. However, now that I am a follower of Jesus Christ, I couldn't do it, and I'm glad that I didn't know the truth until now. I'll mark that up to another of the numerous times that God decided to save my life. Think about that also! A bad decision like I just explained will determine the remainder of your life.

About the Author

As a teen, Charles Elwyn left his NJ home and his verbally and emotionally abusive father for the streets of NYC where he experienced gang life as a member of the Park Rats. Before long he had associated with the Genovese crime family, where he worked in the trucking business as a truck driver and advanced to being the manager of two trucking companies and as a collector. His atheist worldview gave him the belief that he would not live long, and alcohol abuse, physical conditioning through the karate martial arts, and adultery became his lifestyle.

He "escaped" from New York after turning thirty and moved to California where he worked in the construction industry as a commercial superintendent. God spoke specifically to him in a miracle while doing a reconstruction of a church, causing him to stop and listen…and search for THE TRUTH.

A move to Lake Tahoe, CA, allowed him to design and build homes as he put together a new life with God, and he met his wife Wendy. He was able to eventually witness to his two children, who both turned to Jesus as well. He and Wendy now live in Santa Fe, New Mexico, after twenty-eight years of marriage as of this writing.

The Cornerstone was where he met Jesus, giving him a desire to share his past in the hope of helping others to avoid the lure of a life of crime.

Visit: chuckelwyn@gmail.com

CPSIA information can be obtained
at www.ICGtesting.com
Printed in the USA
LVHW110300120522
718586LV00006B/94

9 781638 748526